Pitkin County Library
120 North Mill Street
Aspen, Colorado 81611

VAN NOSTRAND REINHOLD MANUALS
GENERAL EDITOR: W.S. TAYLOR

Film-making

Barry Callaghan

Van Nostrand Reinhold
Manual of **Film-making**

VNR **VAN NOSTRAND REINHOLD COMPANY**
New York Cincinnati Toronto London Melbourne

The author wishes to thank David J. Baker for valuable and substantial help in the preparation of this book. The diagrams on p. 47 are adapted, by permission, from *The Craft of Film* (ed. J.D. Fisher), Attic Publishing Co., 1970. For permission to reproduce film stills, acknowledgments are due to Contemporary Films Ltd (pages 54 above, 71 right, 77, 78), Connoisseur Films Ltd (page 83), Cinema International Corporation (page 74), Columbia-Warner (page 73), M.C.A. (page 54 below), R.K.O. Radio Pictures Ltd (page 75), United Artists Corporation (page 55).

Van Nostrand Reinhold Company
Regional Offices: New York
Cincinnati Chicago Millbrae Dallas

Van Nostrand Reinhold Company
International Offices: London
Toronto Melbourne

Copyright © 1973 by Thames and
Hudson Ltd, London
Library of Congress Catalog Card
Number 73-14114
ISBN 0-442-21445-6 (cloth)
    0-442-21446-4 (paper)

Printed in Great Britain by
Jarrold and Sons Ltd, Norwich

Published in the U.S.A. in 1974 by
Van Nostrand Reinhold Company
A Division of Litton Educational
Publishing, Inc. 450 West 33rd
Street, New York N.Y. 10001

16 15 14 13 12 11 10 9 8 7 6 5 4 3 2 1

Contents

Introduction

This book is written to provide a comprehensive introduction to the technique of film-making for a person making his first film under professional or semi-professional conditions. Student film-makers in their first and perhaps second years, newcomers to professional or semi-professional film production units, and advanced amateur film-makers who have access to well-equipped facilities are the people this book chiefly aims to help. People approaching their first serious film, with little or no knowledge of technique, have often felt that existing film instruction manuals have been mostly rather above their heads and have not differentiated between essential first items of information and more refined techniques, which may be beyond the grasp or needs of the novice film-maker, and that although giving all of (and more than) the necessary information, they have not given a very clear picture of how to put that information into practice. This book tries to bear both of these considerations in mind, and, while giving as much basic technical information as is necessary to complete a straightforward film, tries to relate the information to the actual process of working through the film. The reader of this book will ideally be continually asking: 'Yes – and what do I do now?'

This is not to say, however, that many existing manuals of film technique are not extremely valuable: indeed, several are referred to in the course of this book, which is designed to be used in conjunction with other, more detailed, books which can fill in many of the inevitable gaps that are inherent in an approach such as the present. In particular, the excellent *The Craft of Film* (ed. J. David Fisher) is strongly recommended as a source of technical information very necessary to complement the use of books such as the present one. Various other works dealing with the several aspects of film technique in fuller detail are mentioned in the text; a selective bibliography is appended.

This book aims to be an introduction, a guide through the initial stages of film-making. It tries to give a clear picture of film technique, and to outline the main areas of working. To do this inevitably means resisting the temptation of going too deeply into particular problems: to do so would unbalance the over-all picture. The need to present the process as a whole precludes detailed analysis of many essential aspects of film-making; these areas must be more fully explored by the film-maker himself, once he has acquired basic confidence in the medium.

The level at which the book is aimed has led to the adoption of as non-technical a language as is possible without sacrificing accurate description and professional standards. Most technical terms likely to be encountered by the film-maker are explained and used as necessary. Film talk can very easily descend to jargon; this has been avoided as much as possible, and technical terms have normally been explained in everyday language.

Certain assumptions have been made, however, and below a certain level explanations and descriptions of equipment and phenomena have not been offered. Descriptions of film splicers, or of lacing paths of editing machines, for example, will not be found. The exceptions to this – such as descriptions of camera, microphones and so forth – are where an understanding of the basic mechanical (or electrical) functioning of the equipment is essential for the operator to get the best use from them.

The book has been divided up into sections merely for convenience of discussion. No area of film-making can exist in isolation from the others, and the technique of each aspect invariably depends in some measure on the technique of the others. Especially in small-unit filming – to which this book primarily addresses itself – several jobs are often done by one man, although in professional, union-approved units, doubling on jobs is strongly discouraged. Therefore the production of a film is considered less in terms of the various stages it goes through, than in terms of a continuous growth. This is a healthy attitude to a film, and to involve, on a broad front, many members of the unit can be valuable – so long, that is, as decisions and responsibilities are taken and accepted in the right places. And, of course, it often happens that a film is made by one man alone; and here a sense of the balance and the interrelation of the broad aspects of film-making must be developed. Editing depends to some extent on camerawork; camerawork on sound; sound on script; and script on the potential of all of them. Although these fields are discussed under different chapter headings, they must never be thought of as separate.

Finally, this book accepts that mistakes can and do occur during the making of a first film. So due emphasis is given to the things most likely to go wrong in the various stages, and to their remedies. Thus the book is devoted to the practice of making a first film, rather than to the more abstract theory of film-making. But the two cannot be separated, and if there is one sound piece of all-purpose advice, that is, see how it has been done before; do not necessarily copy the techniques, but see them in action, note, accept or reject, or earmark as a starting point for development. And all the time, more information may well be going in unnoticed than ever gets remembered consciously. Film is a very involving and demanding medium, and for consistent success, the film-maker must be prepared to put in continuous and very hard work.

1 Organization and setting up

In all film-making, careful planning at the early stages of the operation saves time, trouble and heartache in the later stages. This often uncomfortable fact cannot be too heavily stressed or too often repeated. The almost innate excitement of all film-makers, even the most experienced, can make the long and often tedious preparations necessary seem a tiresome chore, to be finished with as soon as possible in order to start on the more rewarding work of scripting, shooting, editing and sound. But the very nature of the medium makes thorough preparation essential: many stages and elements make up a film, and the success of each depends to a greater or lesser extent on the success of all the others. Further, because of the length of time over which the film-making process extends, and because of the unrepeatable nature of much of the work (for reasons of expense, subject availability and time), an ill-prepared or botched job in any one department of the film remains with the film-maker for a long time, and will have a detrimental effect on the finished work. However good the sound-track, editing and acting of a film may be, the total effect of the film will be poor if the camerawork is shoddy. A shot taken on a distant location, marred by poor colour or poor exposure because the cameraman had forgotten to take with him the correct filter, may well be indispensable to the structure of the film, and keep reminding the editor – possibly the same man – of the lack of organization that led to its failure. And what is more, the audience will notice it too. It is worth remembering that once the shot has been taken, the film-maker is stuck with it; it is far better to make that extra bit of effort at the end of a long, hard day's shooting, than for the following three months to regret the five minutes saved. A carefully prepared script will ensure efficient shooting; carefully logged and labelled picture and sound rushes will help smooth editing; carefully prepared locations and well-chosen equipment will ensure good-quality sound recording; and all preparation will save time.

The setting up of a film falls broadly into two areas – the organization of ideas and the organization of facilities. The organization of facilities to ensure the smooth translation of the script into a completed film is the concern of this section. The organization of the ideas constitutes the scripting of the film, and this is dealt with in the next chapter.

Organization of facilities can be grouped under four heads: equipment; the location, or studio; personnel; finance.

EQUIPMENT

It is essential that all equipment necessary for a shooting session be on hand, and all contingencies should be planned for when organizing equipment, especially for location shooting. An analysis of equipment necessary is the first requirement. Heavy lighting, for instance, will not often be needed for exteriors, whereas a small sun-gun may be useful. Especially where equipment must be transported, an accurate forecast of needs will pay dividends.

Checklists should be made – or consulted – to ensure that small items that may be overlooked during rushed loading are not forgotten. It is probably as well to have checklists for each group of equipment, e.g., a camera checklist, a lighting checklist, a sound checklist. Checklists will be compiled by each individual film unit according to their equipment, but a camera checklist, for example, may look like this:

Camera
Lenses
Tripod, head and spreader
Shoulder pod
Baby-legs

Tripod adapter
Cable release
Lens hood
Filter holders
Filters

Selvyt cloth
Lens brush
Batteries and cables
Magazines
Changing bag
Camera report sheets
Spirit level
Pan viewing filter

Blower brush
Cores and spools

Camera tape
Felt-tip pen
Carrying cases
Simple tools –
screwdrivers, pliers
Grey card
Filmstock
Spare cans
Blanking caps and lens caps
Exposure meter and
accessories
Tissues
String
Clapper-board
Chalk
Duster
Matte box and mattes
Tape measure
Waterproof equipment
cover

Lighting and sound checklists should be compiled in similar detail, and all should be checked before the shooting session.

Except in very well-equipped film units, it may be occasionally necessary to rent certain items of equipment. In small-unit 16-mm. production, renting of equipment can be a significant part of the budget; renting should be carefully considered, and time allocated so as to make fullest use of the equipment during the period of rent. A sound camera and recorder (such as the Arriflex BL and Nagra III), essential for shooting synchronous sound, may cost £35 per day to rent: in a budget of a few hundred pounds this can be a significant item of expenditure.

As with other production services – labs, dubbing studios etc. – it is worth while establishing contact with one rental firm, and using their services regularly. Since much film equipment is very expensive and delicate, rental firms are often apprehensive about renting equipment to new clients without adequate proof of competence, and rightly so. Further, when a film-maker is renting equipment, he needs an absolutely reliable service: arrangements cannot be held up because of non-arrival, or poor state of rented equipment. A good rental service will also ensure that equipment is delivered complete with all necessary accessories, and sometimes a stock of consumables is provided as well. When renting, make sure that terms of business, conditions, costs, transport and insurance arrangements are fully understood beforehand, and remember that most firms will need reasonable notice – particularly with larger items – to guarantee availability.

Be absolutely clear as to what equipment is required: large rental firms have a considerable range of equipment available, and some types of camera, for instance, may be more suited to certain kinds of work than others. It is pointless renting an Arriflex BL if all shooting is to be mute, and an Arriflex S, at a much lower charge, will do the job equally well. And be sure there is someone on the unit who is fully acquainted with the specific item: cameras, for example, can be very different in design and operation. A tightly-organized shooting session is no time to make first acquaintance with a complicated piece of film equipment, and there are obvious dangers of ruined footage and of damage to the camera.

Consumable material – chiefly filmstock and magnetic recording tape – must be accurately estimated. A good stock of reserve should be allowed, to cover unexpected opportunities, retakes, mishaps, technical errors and so forth. The type of filmstock will probably have been decided at the shooting-script stage; but if possible, tests should also be carried out to ensure that no factors have been overlooked in the original selection of stock. As a simple example of this, the estimated lighting for an indoor location might prove impracticable, and a faster film than at first suggested might prove necessary. A visit to the location before shooting will give the necessary information, but where this is not possible, or in cases of doubt, alternative filmstocks should be taken.

The organization of equipment for a film does not stop at the successful arrangement of a shooting session. Before the first foot is shot, ascertain that the facilities to handle the processed footage are to hand. Is a cutting-room available for the estimated time of editing? Is the cutting-room fully equipped to handle all the shot film and sound? If sync footage is to be cut, for example, is there access to a picture synchronizer and an editing-machine or table? Is double-head projection possible? Will the production unit require master cutting facilities, or will this work be entrusted to a cutting service?

Familiarize yourself with the laboratories and sound studios to be used, as these will play a vital role in the completion of the film. It is necessary to be certain that your labs can handle the type of filmstock being used, and that the quality of their work is up to the standards required. Learn their preferred system of marking up and presentation of work; this will help them to give efficient service. The labs chosen should be able to do any kind of duplicating, printing and optical work that may be necessary to the film, and carry out any other services. A clear definition of requirements, and a close liaison with the firm chosen, will ensure that all lab work is carried out smoothly.

Finally, transport must be arranged, not only to deliver equipment and personnel to locations, but also for collection of equipment, delivery of work to labs, and attendance of appropriate members of the editing team at grading conferences, dubbing sessions and so forth.

THE LOCATION OR STUDIO

Organization for studio filming with small-unit 16-mm. production should be straightforward. Apart from television work, comparatively little is done in anything other than a small studio organized professionally to meet the needs of its users. Preparation for studio work will thus be chiefly concerned with finding and hiring the studio, and a thorough check of its resources in relation to the sequences to be shot. Any shortcomings in the studio's facilities should be made up when equipment is being arranged, though, in addition to the provision of technical equipment, fittings, props and so on must be made available as and when required. For indoor work not in a properly equipped professional studio, organizational problems will be similar to some of those encountered with location filming, with the addition of special considerations such as the provision of materials for props and fittings.

Location filming, where the situation is not directly under the control of the film unit, and where the film-maker must adapt to the circumstances, presents problems of organization and must be thoroughly prepared if the required amount of work is to be produced in the time available. The best solution is for the film-maker to visit the location in advance of filming, to assess the advantages and drawbacks of the situation, and to adapt his script and shooting schedule to what he finds. If such a visit is impossible, contact should be established with somebody at or near the location who can answer detailed questions about it, and who can act as a liaison officer for the scene. An obvious example is the public relations officer of a firm for which a film is being made, or the manager responsible for commissioning the film: if there is someone with filmic or photographic knowledge at the scene, so much the better.

Location work can include both interior and exterior shooting, and can cover both controlled and uncontrolled action. With controlled action, where the director can stage every shot as he is ready to shoot, and can consider refinements on the shooting script, or alternative ways of shooting a take, the technique may be similar to that of studio production. But the location itself will certainly not be fitted out for film-making. You should therefore concentrate on making the best use of such facilities as do exist. First, the unit will want a room to use as a base, where equipment can be stored and kept clear of the shooting area, which may well be severely limited anyway. Secondly, for most interior locations, lighting of some kind will be used; the electricity supply must be confirmed, and in many cases an electrician will be needed. If Colortran lighting – very widely used by all kinds of film unit – is needed, a supply of 30 or even 40 amps may be required. A supply of this nature is not often easy to find, and an electrician will usually be essential, to wire the lighting supply direct from a mains panel. If a sufficient supply of electricity is not available on the location, modified or altered lighting arrangements will have to be made. Thirdly, the location must be assessed for camera and lighting positions, and for sound-recording possibilities. Is there enough floor space to make use of a camera dolly? Will normal and/or short tripods, or table-mounts, be required for the camera? Will a shoulder harness be needed to get the required angles of some subjects? Lamp stands may clutter up limited space, and polecats or existing supports can be utilized. Will amber gels or blue filters be needed to even out mixed light sources? If any sound recording other than guide tracks is to be done on the location, the acoustic character of the room should be assessed and, if necessary, improved.

In uncontrolled filming, a thorough assessment of the location is even more important. Where the cameraman must shoot a once-off, unrepeatable action while it is happening, with no chance for retakes – a procession, perhaps, or a sporting event – practical questions such as camera positions, lighting, and suchlike, must be decided beforehand as there will often be no chance of changing them once the shooting has begun. For large-scale outdoor events, envisage the scene as well as possible, and make arrangements for the best camera positions in advance. High vantage points, such as the roof of a large building, or positions on a private piece of land must be negotiated for, and the need for extra camera operators – perhaps with a hand-held camera or perhaps with a camera to shoot cutaways – must be considered. Permits or photographers' passes may be required to shoot in certain locations, and should be obtained in advance; local police regulations about photography in public places should also be mastered. The question of release permits (written permission to use footage including well-known or professional people, for example) may have to be examined. Thoughtful preparation of uncontrolled exterior filming will pay dividends: without it many good shots may well be missed. Unlike controlled location work, the fresh idea that occurs while filming may prove impossible to realize, solely because of organizational difficulties. The spectre of an editor moaning 'if only . . .' often haunts film studios.

Other considerations for location shooting generally include alternative arrangements in case of unsuitable weather (with the complications of location shooting, a day lost through rain may prove expensive in time, and possibly hire of equipment: forethought may make it possible to shoot an alternative scene on what would otherwise have been a wasted day); estimation of time required for the scene (it is too easy to underestimate, and setting up of equipment alone can make large claims on hoped-for shooting time); and of course the provision of transport and facilities such as food and shelter for the personnel involved.

Especially on a distant location, the emphasis on planning cannot be too heavily stressed. A careless shot at the end of a day, a shot missed because the camera was not in the right place at the right time, a vital part of the operation not covered well enough in the footage shot – all will leave their mark on the finished film. The editor can only work with what the camera crew bring back with them.

PERSONNEL

Every single person involved in any way with the shooting of a scene must be at all times fully aware of what is going on and of what is required of him. Filming is too complex and expensive an operation for a whole unit to be held up for two hours because an electrician has not turned up, or because a factory manager has forgotten that this was the day that the scene was to be filmed. It is the film-maker's responsibility to see that all people involved are aware of, and reminded, perhaps on the day prior to shooting, of what is necessary. It is only too easy to set up a scene, say, demonstrating some technical process, only to find that the only man capable of operating a vital piece of ancillary equipment has gone away to a one-day conference, and is unobtainable; or to set up a dramatic scene with five extras of whom (especially if unpaid) three fail to materialize – each assuming there will be four others left, and that they will do. It is also important to ensure that there is an appropriate person available to do any job that may prove necessary. Hoping that 'someone will be around' who has the talents or qualifications needed is unsafe in film-making, and time and goodwill (in itself a not inconsiderable asset in location work) can easily be lost searching around for someone to stand in. The philosophy of 'it'll have to do' has no place in film-making.

FINANCE

Nearly every 16-mm. film is made to a budget, from a student's first exercise to a full-scale prestige or television production costing tens of thousands of pounds. Since the money available has very far-reaching effects on the final nature of the film, the financial organization should be very carefully worked out.

The kind of budget a film gets depends obviously on the type of film, and the purpose for which it is made. The position of the film unit, the number of outside services it has to call on, the extent of overheads and professional fees will all have their effect on the final figure. Whereas the professional film unit's budget will very largely be taken up by such things as overheads, wages, depreciation etc., the budget of a student film may be almost exclusively devoted to raw materials, and laboratory and sound-studio charges. The first requirement, then, is to establish what must be paid for from the finance of the film, and to apportion the money available to the best advantage of the film.

Items common to all budgets will be raw materials, laboratory and sound-laboratory charges, and hire fees, if necessary. The following are typical items that might go towards making up the materials side of a budget:

Raw materials

The cost of *filmstock* will vary according to the stock used, especially between black-and-white and colour. The amount of film used will depend not only on the total length of the projected film, but also on the nature of the subject, and the degree of control the director has. With a well-planned technical film, it may be possible to use almost all the footage shot: with uncontrolled filming it may be necessary to shoot five, or even twenty times the final running time of the film. Furthermore, special stocks may be needed for particular purposes – high-contrast stocks for titling, for example.

Remember when estimating amounts of *magnetic recording tape* required that it is not consumed at the same rate as picture film – more or less may be required, according to circumstances.

Black spacing is essential in master assembly (A & B roll), and, since it is as costly as filmstock, it should not be overlooked in budgeting.

Assorted *leader* and *spacing* required at various stages, particularly track-laying.

Sundries – several small items required during editing.

Laboratory charges

Processing. The lab will provide a complete price list of all costs, reckoned by the foot. Note that forced and other special processing is more costly than normal processing. The decision whether to use neg./pos. or reversal stock will also affect processing and print costs, and must be taken into account.

Rush print, for cutting-copy.

Approval and release prints. Charges here will vary according to a number of factors: printing from A and B rolls, colour correction and grading, fades and dissolves produced in printing, printing of optical sound-tracks – these will all add to the cost of prints. Approval and single copies are also more expensive than subsequent copies: most labs have a scale of charges, reduced as the number of copies increases.

Optical printing for special effects – freeze-frames, image placement, reverse and stretch printing, for example – is expensive. An initial setting-up charge is usually made before the actual cost, charged by the foot, is calculated.

Negative or positive master for the optical sound-track.

Magnetic striping of the film, if sound is to be magnetic.

Additional services – such as master inspection, negative cutting, waxing of print, scratch treatment and so on – may be necessary.

Sound studio charges

Sound transfer from $\frac{1}{4}$-in. magnetic tape to 16-mm. magnetic film. The charge for this normally includes the price of the virgin stock.

Hire of the dubbing theatre for the mixing of the tracks. This is charged for by the hour, and includes the services of the dubbing mixer. Allow for at least three times the running time of the film – even more if the tracks are complicated, or if any difficulty is foreseen.

Final transfer to magnetic stripe, for magnetic sound copies. This should only take the running time of the film, but setting-up time must also be allowed.

Studio time for recording commentary to film.

As noted earlier, *hire charges* can be high in a small budget, and if equipment is to be hired, efficient use should be made of it. Hire firms will supply their price list.

Additions to these basic budgeting requirements will vary from unit to unit, and items such as wages, overheads, depreciation of equipment, professional fees, commentator's fees, transport, overtime, insurance, copyright fees and other clearances, script-writer's and animator's fees, must be costed according to the position of the individual film unit.

When the over-all picture of the approved budget is clear, the money available for the basic production materials must be analysed in relation to the script of the film. At this stage, the amount of money available can materially affect the entire construction of an approach to the film. Organizational and filmic priorities may now be in conflict: can colour be afforded, and if not, can it be dropped without seriously impairing the impact of the film? Does a freeze-frame written into the script really justify its cost, in relation to the over-all cost of the film? Will the money available allow for the amount of shooting estimated as essential in the script? Is synchronous sound essential to a scene, or could the sequence be equally effectively done with wild sound, and the cost of hiring expensive equipment saved?

On all but the very simplest of films, the organization and setting-up process is a major and integral part of the finished product. Often, though, the planning of the film can seem, except marginally, to be an uncreative labour to be hurried through in order to get on to the actual construction of the film itself, and as such to be passed over lightly, especially in informal film units. But the organization of the film is in fact one of the vital keys to its success. A good script, sensitive and imaginative direction, gripping camerawork, editing and sound are some of the obvious qualities that commend a film to its audience. But none of these is sufficient in isolation – indeed slackness in only one of these departments can seriously impair a film's quality; it is only by perceptive and thoughtful planning that, given individual skills and talent, the several aspects of a film's creation can be consistently and successfully brought together. Like the proverbial hour's sleep before midnight, an hour's planning before shooting begins may well be worth two hours afterwards.

2 The script

The script is the cinematic and practical embodiment of the idea of the film, and the arrangements indicated in the previous chapter cannot be fully settled without the preparation of the script. A well-prepared script is a major part of the setting-up of the film, and it is probably the most obviously creative part of pre-shooting work. The main function of the script is to supply the most thorough filmic consideration of the idea that the film will pass through. In most cases the over-all balance of the film, its main lines of thought, its emphases and a good part of the actual shot-to-shot construction will be decided at this stage.

The script is not only creative in relation to the more abstract aspects of the film – the ideas it contains, the attitudes it expresses – but also in the concrete cinematic expression that will give the film its identity. The disposition of long-shots, medium-shots and close-ups will be established; the rhythm of the editing will be indicated; effective camera angles and provisions for cutting points will be considered; the interrelation of the action and sound-track will be estimated; special effects will be specified, and many similar considerations will be thoroughly worked out. The real importance of creative thinking at the script stage is that it is then that it is possible to take a clear view of the film, undistracted by shot material, and to make considered formal decisions as to its over-all construction, the development of its main ideas, and the way in which the filmic construction will embody these ideas. This is not, however, to deny that there is room for creative thinking at shooting and editing stages: obviously, detailed amendments and improvements will be made to the script during the making of the film; often the script can only indicate general ideas, and major decisions of all kinds will have to be taken while shooting and editing.

The following are only examples of the kind of areas that may have to be examined during the preparation of the script: each film will have its own specific requirements, and the script will reflect the individual nature of the film.

The idea and story. An original idea will need to be fully worked and prepared for expression in the film medium. An adapted idea may have to be substantially restructured to make it suitable for film form. With documentary material, an attitude and means of presentation must be established; with technical material, suitable means of demonstration must be found.

The length of the film. The length of time needed to put across the chosen interpretation of the idea should be envisaged, or alternatively, how best to film the required idea or information in a given time. A twenty-minute film is a different proposition from a twenty-two-minute film.

Balance of film. Within the over-all length of the film, how are the sequences to be ordered and balanced to achieve the desired effect? The relative importance and length of the various sequences; the rhythmic shape of the film and its sequences; disposition of crises and emphases, and how these will affect the audience's reaction to the film.

The choice of filmstock and the visual appearance of the film. How will the visual surface of the film affect the audience's reaction to the content of the film? Black-and-white or colour? Grainy images or fine-grain? Contrasty, or with full tonal range? Hand-held sequences? Ideas about camerawork and composition? High-key and/or low-key lighting?

Special effects. Special effects draw the audience's attention, and so must be carefully used. Mattes, slow-motion, split-screen etc. must be considered from the script stage. All cinematic expression requires forethought, and special effects in particular must be an integral part of the structure of the film, rather than an ornamental afterthought.

Editing patterns. Although the script-writer can hardly shackle an editor to preconceived notions about the detailed cutting of the film, he must visualize the broad pattern of the editor's work. The nature of the editing has a powerful influence on the appearance of the completed piece of work and its effect on an audience, and the script-writer must calculate for this in thinking about the film. Is a particular scene to be cut with a fast and exciting rhythm, or a slow and leisurely one? Is the editor to be allowed to experiment with eyelines, continuity and so forth so as to heighten the impact of a certain sequence? Exactly what is the editor's involvement in the construction of the film to be? In a purely technical and closely scripted film, his main job may be only to find the right cutting points in an unalterable sequence of shots, while in a dramatic action scene or montage sequence he may be freer to decide what shots to use and the positioning and length of those shots. What use is likely to be made of cutaways and reaction shots?

The sound-track. The sound-track must be as thoroughly thought out as the visual aspects of the film. Decisions on what kind of sound to use and how to use it, must be taken at script stage. Will a certain scene have to be shot sync, or would a wild track with voiceover be more telling? Is a music track necessary, and if so, how will it be best used? How elaborate must the effects track be? How will the sound be edited, and how will it contribute to the editing of the action? How long will be needed for a commentary to impart its essential information, and will it underline, or complement, the action? Are special sound effects wanted, and justifiable?

Actors, extras, costume, location, studio, sets and many other items for consideration will also appear at the scripting stage of various kinds of film. Details of all such requirements, and their integration into the film, must be decided before the film is shot.

The script is a major creative part of the film, and must be recognized as such. With fully controlled subjects, the film is to a large extent made in the scripting stage. Even with uncontrolled subjects, as thorough a script as possible will enable the camera crew to take fullest advantage of the opportunities. A good director, cameraman and editor can make poorly scripted material presentable: but the best craftsmen and artists in the world cannot make a good film from a poor script.

There are five generally recognized stages in the preparation of a film script: the idea and first draft; treatment; screenplay or scenario; shooting script; shooting schedule.

THE IDEA AND FIRST DRAFT

This is perhaps not a well defined stage of script-writing; but before the writer presents his treatment, he will clearly have to spend much time in general consideration of the film. If the subject of the film is imposed on the writer, he will need to assemble his ideas about how it should be turned into a film; he will need to research the background to his subject, and probably to discuss the needs, aims and contents of the film with its producer. If the subject is of the writer's own choice, the creative assembly of ideas – or the selection of the source for an adaptation – will need much work before the writer is in a position to produce the treatment. On the one hand, work at this stage of the script may be no more than discussion with the parties involved in the film; on the other, it may appear as sheafs of personal notes, suggestions of alternatives, or even trial sequences actually shot. The method will depend both on the type of film involved and on the individual script-writer.

THE TREATMENT

The treatment is a fairly brief prose description of how the writer sees the film. It will normally concentrate on the content of the film, and will only broadly indicate the filmic interpretation of the subject. The structure of the film will be generally suggested, but the filmic details of individual sequences will not be elaborated. General practical observations will be included – estimated running time, how many, and which, actors, general locations and so forth. With a sponsored film, the treatment will be submitted for approval before work starts on the screenplay.

At this stage the treatment is broken down into sequences, and analysed with a view to its expression in film form. The individual style of the film begins to emerge. The dialogue is written in, as well as the commentary, general sound effects and other sound-track matter. Details of the locations, interiors and exteriors, day or night sequences are all indicated. The individual scenes are constructed; the dramatic and/or filmic shape of the film is now clearly specified, and the atmosphere of the film should be quite clearly conveyed. The screenplay, in fact, is that stage of the script at which the film is most clearly described to a reader: earlier stages are too brief and general, while later phases are perhaps too full of technical details and instructions for a reader to be able to grasp the flow of the ideas, and to envisage the effect of the film. The practice of publishing screenplays of well-known films, rather than their shooting scripts, exemplifies this.

THE SHOOTING SCRIPT

This is the complete, detailed breakdown of the film into shot-by-shot order, anticipating every shot that will be used, and how that shot will look. Every action and scene of the screenplay will be described in terms of individual shots: details will include type of shot (LS, MS, CU etc.), lens to be used, camera angles, lighting patterns, subject movements and camera movements, even, possibly, cutting points. A story-board – really a visual presentation of the shooting script, with drawings taking the place of shot descriptions – may also be prepared at this point. In theory the test of a well-prepared shooting script is that if it is given to a competent director, cameraman and editor, they should be able to deliver a film that is very close in actuality to the script-writer's intention. In practice, of course, this does not happen: most directors and cameramen are not content to be merely competent, and in most cases the director works very closely with the script-writer, if indeed he is not the same man.

Suppose the film-maker is working on an idea for a film about a miner on his last day of work after fifty-three years in the pits. He has been thinking the idea over for some months, and has made notes, and has a clear picture of what he wants to say. The successive stages of the script will finalize his ideas, perhaps, as follows:

Treatment. The film will look at some of the traditional hardships and injustices of the miner's life through the life in the pits of one man, who has worked in a colliery since he left school at the age of twelve. A certain amount of archive material will be incorporated in the film, but by and large reconstruction will not be used as a method

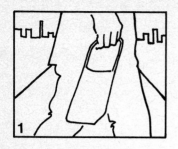

Storyboard sketch.

of presentation. Instead, Mr Blank will recount stories of the old days – some of the time in sync interview, some of the time in voiceover – and his stories will be illustrated by their modern counterparts, with shots of the present colliery workings. The general attitude to the film will be as neutral as possible . . . etc.

Screenplay. Scene 1. Outside the colliery, early morning. Jack, the subject of the film, is walking down the hill towards the main gate. He stops briefly, and looks over the colliery. The miners are walking down the road in groups of two and three: the early-morning sun lights up the white helmets, and the smoke from the big chimneys. The sounds of the pit are still fairly distant. As he watches, his face impassive, the siren for the end of the previous shift blasts suddenly. Jack starts slightly, and moves on down the road. Commentary starts: 'Thing-ummy pit, opened in 1849 . . .'.

The same sequence could also be drawn, as the *story-board*, in some such way as shown on the left.

Alternatively, the shooting script may be laid out in a more formal manner in a sheet of paper ruled into columns:

Shot no.	Shot	Action	Sound-track	Remarks
1	CU	Jack's snap-tin swinging as he walks.	Natural sounds, early a.m. outside colliery. Jack's footsteps heard going over cobbles.	FADE IN at beginning. Hold for some time.

The shooting schedule. This is strictly an administrative rather than a scripting job, and represents the breakdown of the shooting script into convenient work sessions for the camera crew. All scenes to be shot on the same location, for example, or all scenes requiring the same actors, will be grouped together for shooting, irrespective of their script order and final position in the film. Estimated time for shooting is included, as well as details of equipment and unit staff needed for the shooting session. In professional and large-unit film-making, a full shooting schedule is necessarily an essential administrative operation. Small units, or the lone film-maker, will obviously not need the same detail of written preparation, as long as the director is capable of organizing things successfully in his head. A shooting schedule might work out like this:

Day 1. Scenes 1, 8, 9, and final scene (17). Location: the colliery, exteriors 1 and 17, interiors 8 and 9. Actors: Jack, four other miners. Equipment: sync camera and recorder; Colortran lights and 2 sun-guns; 2nd camera mute, 2nd tape-recorder for effects and background; camera dolly. Note: Contact electrician and section manager for interior shooting. . . .

And so forth, including all details, from permits to changing-rooms, of the anticipated day's shooting.

These then are the first stages in the preparation of the film script. It should be noted that the stages outlined are theoretical, the completed process of script-writing: elaborate development of each stage is a counsel of perfection. In point of fact, many good short films made by individuals or small groups do not have scripts as thoroughly prepared as this; a film can be quite successfully made from a story-board alone, or even from a treatment if the script-writer is also the director. Furthermore, it should be added that there are many kinds of film subject that do not lend themselves to rigorous planning in advance: once-off events, newsreel sequences, live interviews, informal occasions, and all those sequences where events and people are not in the control of the director, none of these can be given as thorough a shooting script as the one outlined above. However, scripting on these occasions is very important, even if it does not take the same form as other scripting. The location, for instance, can be visited, and notes made on how it can best be used to the film's advantage; the good camera positions it offers; the angles which will make best use of it. Programmes can be obtained to give some idea about the nature and duration of the events; background information can be sought on people to be interviewed; and much other work can be done in preparation which will pay dividends in well-shot and sufficient material. A well-prepared film – whatever the detailed method of preparation – is well on the way to being a well-made film.

Outlined above is a guide to the preparation of a film script. But what goes into the script, and how the proposed content of the film is adapted for cinematic presentation, is even more important to the film. Unfortunately, an entire volume would hardly be enough to discuss this question, which includes all branches of film aesthetics and criticism: a question in fact that revolves around the whole of the film-maker's ideas on what film is. A discourse on this topic is clearly beyond the scope of this book; there are, however, a number of relevant questions and decisions that can be proposed; these most script-writers – and indeed directors – will encounter at some stage during the film.

The problem can be quite simply expressed as a two-part question: what is the film (or the scene) saying (or doing)? What is the best way to say or do this in cinematic terms? The first part of the question must be readily answered by the film-maker, otherwise there is no film. The second part needs much work and thought. As a brief illustration – it can be no more – of some of the things to be taken into consideration, let us look at one small section of a hypothetical script. Assuming that the subject and structure of the film have been decided upon, the scene now being worked

23

on is of a man sitting at a table writing: after a short time he gets up, walks to the window and looks out.

This simple bit of action can be covered cinematically in anything from one to fifty (or even more) shots, and each of these shots can be one of an infinitely variable number of possibilities. The number and kind of shots chosen will depend upon all kinds of factors: the nature of the film, the nature of the sequence within the film, the importance of the scene within the sequence, the complexity of the sound-track, and a host of similar circumstances. All of these must be weighed up before the decisions are taken. In addition there are a number of cinematic factors that will remain constant throughout the scene, perhaps throughout the film, that must also be determined. The lighting of the scene, which has a most important bearing on the total effect, must be chosen (high key or low key, for example), and the photographic quality (granularity, black-and-white or colour, filters, special effects and so on), which is also crucial, must be specified.

The different ways of scripting and shooting this scene result from the following variables: number of shots; type of shots (LS, CU etc); length of shots; content of shots; angle of shot; composition of shot; camera movement; subject movement; rhythm of editing; the sound-track. These must be combined, by the judgment and experience of the script-writer, to produce the effect that is most fitting for the particular film.

For the sample scene, assume that an even, high-key lighting set-up has been chosen, colour filmstock specified, with no special visual effects. A few of the infinite number of ways in which this might be shot are:

In one shot. Even with a single shot for the whole action, there is still a great number of variables. Is a stationary LS, for example, better than a moving CU, or will the latter have more impact? Is impact what is needed in the scene, or is the action a mere routine movement of ordinary narrative content, needing unemphatic camerawork and direction? Does the shot have to show any particular quality of the subject – he may be a vampire – or is his nature either already well established or else insignificant? Is a zoom or a tracking shot likely to be effective in the circumstances? Are there any significant details of the room that the shot should emphasize, by framing, movement or other means? Is a high camera angle or a low one likely to serve the needs of the scene best? Where will the camera best be placed? Remember that virtually every cubic inch of space within the room represents a different camera position, and though it is strictly the cameraman's task finally to decide the exact cubic inch his lens will occupy, the script-writer must also take responsibility – say to the cubic foot. The script-writer must conceptualize the scene: the cameraman realizes it.

In three shots. The questions that posed themselves to the script-writer about the single shot now present themselves three times. It is worth noting at this point that the choice of the number of shots is not made in isolation from the use of individual shots: the shots needed may require the use of certain others, or the mood suggested by particular shots may in turn suggest other shots. With three shots, the individual interrelation of shots must be considered, as must the total cumulative effect. Are the three shots to be LS – CU – LS, for example, with the CU giving some detail between two straightforward descriptive long-shots, or will the three shots all be CUS, perhaps helping to impart a mood of tension? Will angles remain neutral, or will all three shots be from, say, a low angle? Here are two examples:

1 MLS $\frac{3}{4}$ rear view, over shoulder view of man sitting at desk writing. Natural sound only – movement of his clothing and scratching of the pen. Subject framed centrally in screen.
2 CU high angle, $\frac{3}{4}$ front view, of the pen as it writes on the paper. The writing stops and the pen is put down gently. Natural sound, with pen sound in CU.
3 MS from just below eye level, from front of desk. Man pushes back chair, and camera pans with his movement to window, pulling out to reveal more of his surroundings as he goes. Natural sound.

1 BCU profile of man's face, background out of focus. He is agitated but concentrating. Off-screen we hear the pen scratching feverishly. In addition to the natural sound there are two or three bleak chords of music.
2 BCU clock, with second hand sweeping round. The ticking of the clock comes into close-up, and continues through next shot.
3 CU man's feet, from floor level, as he pushes back chair and walks quickly to window: camera then tilts up to give extremely low-angle view of man, distorted by wide-angle lens. A rattle at the door-knob on the sound-track.

Many more ways of scripting the same action in three shots can readily be imagined. It is the script-writer's job to decide, from all the variables, which is the right one for the film. Five, ten or fifteen shots may well be needed to achieve the best effect. Cutaway shots, significant details, all aspects of acting must be considered, even down to details of framing. A CU of a head with a clock in the background may be more telling or appropriate than the same head with an indeterminate background: a difference that could be achieved by moving the camera by a mere few inches.

Many films will, further, need a written script – commentary, dialogue and any other form of controlled spoken work used on the sound-track. The success of the spoken script will clearly depend to a large extent upon the verbal skills of the writer, and this is not the place to discuss written and spoken style at any length. However, there are a few points worth bearing in mind when writing commentary, whether informative or atmospheric, for a film.

First, it is as well to note that a commentary script, when written down, may look rather exaggerated in style. A language of commentary has evolved, and an audience will take for granted many flowery phrases and images that would appear excessive when written down or used in everyday speech. It is merely a heightened form of presentation.

Second, a commentary will not need to fill all the film time available. Short sections of commentary, spaced out with music, effects and perhaps even with other voice tracks, will usually be more effective than an uninterrupted blanket of information. A speaking rate of between two and three words per second is usual with commentators of a professional standard, and this can be taken as a rough guide when estimating the length of a written script.

Third, information is best imparted as concisely as possible. In addition the information given should complement, rather than describe the picture. There is no need to tell the audience what it can see for itself.

Although it is quite possible to write and record a commentary to a completed picture, it is far preferable to evolve the picture and the script of the commentary at the same time. If the commentary and picture are scripted together, there is always latitude to extend or condense and to achieve harmony between the two. Once the picture is finished, the rigid timing enforced upon the commentary script may cramp the writer's style considerably.

Finally, the power of the commentary should not be underestimated; exactly the same piece of film can be completely altered in tone merely by changing the mood of the commentary. The same information can be conveyed in the same time in any number of ways: by choosing the right tone and style the script-writer ensures that the film as a whole turns out the way he envisages it.

In short, to write a successful script, the script-writer must be conversant with almost all aspects of film-making, and must be able to visualize the particular needs of each process. He must think like a director in the proportioning of the film and about its content; he must think like a cameraman in anticipating the visual structuring of each shot; he must think like an editor in predicting the pace of the film and the individual sequences, in providing strong cutting points, and in using the communicative power of editing technique; he must think like a sound editor in the use of his sound effects and dialogue. And, finally, he must react like an audience, so as to judge the final effect of his film. However he works, the script-writer is of fundamental importance to the film. Without the script, in one form or another, there is no film.

3 The camera

The movie camera is the basic tool of the film-maker, and because the actual working of the camera itself is important to the results it produces, it is important to understand its chief principles of operation. Descriptions of movie cameras are given in most technical manuals of film-making, and the handbook supplied with each camera will provide particular details; a brief résumé of points common to all movie cameras, of the features that need to be understood for successful camera operation, will suffice here.

A camera is a light-tight box which allows light to fall on an area of sensitized material (normally film) in a controlled manner, so allowing a latent photographic image to be formed on that sensitized material. The light passes through a lens, which trains the light precisely on to the required area of film, causing the image to be registered in sharp focus; the lens usually has adjustable functions allowing the operator to control the amount of light passing through it. Movie cameras must also be provided with a film transport system, since the effect of motion on the screen is produced by a rapid succession of photographic images recorded and projected at a rate of many images per second.

The film transport system comprises a motor, a feed and take-up system and an intermittent mechanism. The speed of the motor, powered either by clockwork or electricity, must be capable of being governed exactly; any variation in its running speed will be reflected in false interpretation of motion when the film is projected at a continuous speed. There would also be slight variations in exposure caused by fluctuating shutter speeds. The feed and take-up system – normally consisting of either daylight loading spools or rechargeable magazines – must supply and take up the film evenly, consistently and without undue stress.

Since the movie film is composed of a series of still images recorded in rapid succession, the film, during its transport, must be held still at the gate – the position where the film is exposed to the light – while the camera's shutter is open, and must be advanced by the space of one frame while the shutter is closed. Thus, instead of continuous movement on the film there is an intermittent motion, with a rapid alternation of still and moving phases. This is usually effected by a claw, with one or more teeth, engaging in the sprocket holes of the film, pulling it down, holding it still while the exposure is made, withdrawing, moving back up to the next

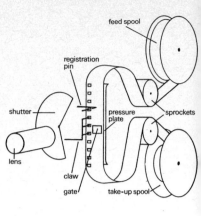

feed spool

registration
pin

shutter

lens

claw

gate

pressure
plate

sprockets

take-up spool

(*Above*) Arri 16 ST camera with
400 ft magazine; (*above*, *right*) typical
camera layout.

(*Below*) The Bolex H16R camera.

sprocket hole(s) and repeating the cycle once for every opening of the shutter. An additional refinement, found on more
expensive cameras, is the inclusion of a register pin which
inserts itself through one sprocket hole during the time of
exposure, and ensures maximum picture steadiness. At
standard sound speed the intermittent cycle takes place 24
times each second, giving 24 photographic images ('frames')
per second, usually written 24 f.p.s. At silent speed there are
16 f.p.s., and at television speed, 25 f.p.s. When these images
are projected with a similar intermittent movement on the
projector, the illusion of movement, dependent on the
retention of the image by the human eye during the brief
period of image replacement ('persistence of vision') that is
essential to film, is created.

The drive of the feed and take-up spools (or the magazine),
however, is continuous, and to avoid stress and damage to the
filmstock by the intermittent movement at the gate, the
film path in the camera incorporates a loop both sides of the
gate. In some cameras the loop is formed automatically
during loading: if this is not the case, great care should always
be taken to ensure the loop is correctly formed. Too small
a loop can result in the film being damaged by stretching and
tearing, as well as interfering with the intermittent mechanism; too large a loop may cause the film to be scratched by
contact with parts of the inside of the camera.

All cameras are provided with a shutter, which prevents
light reaching the film at all times except when the exposure
is being made. On movie cameras shutters are invariably
of a rotating action: a disk with a section cut away – usually
in the region of 170° – rotates on a spindle between the film
in the gate and the light falling through the lens. When the
solid section of the shutter is in front of the gate no light can
pass, and when the cutaway section passes, the exposure is
made. The rotating spindle is geared to the intermittent
claw mechanism so that light is cut off during the downward
pull of the film, and allowed to pass in the time the film is
held still in the gate.

Some cameras are equipped with a variable shutter, which allows the operator to select the angle of opening of the shutter. For example, a cameraman might find himself in conditions that would result in overexposure of the film-stock loaded, even with the smallest lens aperture in use. A variable shutter would then enable him to reduce time of exposure by closing the angle of opening: a fixed shutter will allow of no variation in exposure time. A variable shutter also allows fades and dissolves to be effected in the camera, though in practice this is seldom done as the accuracy necessary in timing the effects cannot easily be foreseen while shooting. Shorter shutter speeds further allow wider lens apertures to be used, which may be desirable to reduce depth of field, or may allow the cameraman to use a mid-range *f*-stop and consequently get the best optical performance from his lens.

Viewfinders are of two chief kinds: reflex and non-reflex. With a reflex viewfinder the image seen in the finder is exactly that to be recorded on the film: the image seen has passed through the lens and by mirror or beam-splitting methods has been presented on the ground-glass screen of the viewer. The advantages of this system are manifest: critical focusing, precise framing and inspection of depth of field are made easy, and the presentation of the image on a ground-glass screen can considerably help the cameraman to visualize the final projected image.

Many cameras, however, have viewfinders that operate by offering an approximation to the lens framing by having a separate attachment on the side or on top of the camera. Used and adjusted properly, these viewfinders can give quite satisfactory results, especially when aided by a reflex focusing system such as that available with the Bolex H 16 S camera. With this system, the taking lens is rotated on its turret into a focusing position, where, in a separate eye-piece, a reflex view through the lens is obtainable, and the lens can be focused precisely and depth of field can be seen. When using this facility, however, great care must be taken to remember to return the lens to the taking position when the shot is taken.

Rackover viewfinders are most commonly found on 35-mm. cameras, although they occasionally feature in 16-mm. work as with the Bolex rackover attachment, which can be used for accurate titling with the non-reflex Bolex. In rackover systems, the whole body of the camera is moved over on its support to allow the non-reflex viewfinder to stand in the exact position that the taking lens will resume when the camera body is returned to taking position. With the Bolex, this allows the reflex focuser to be used in aligning and focusing the shot.

Lenses are fitted to all cameras to focus the light on to the appropriate area of the film, and to produce images of maximum sharpness. Lenses are of several types, and are loosely described by the angle of view which they offer: standard lenses, which approximate to the normal angle of

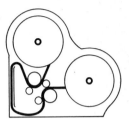

Typical threading path.

Threading path with magazine.

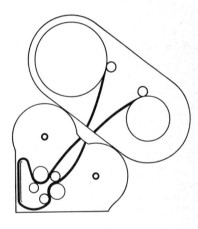

vision of the human eye; wide-angle, which describes any of the lenses that give a wider field of view than standard; and long-focus and telephoto lenses, which give a closer view than standard, having a magnifying effect similar to that of a telescope. Variable-focus, or 'zoom', lenses have an adjustable main element, which enables them to be altered to give wide-angle, standard or telephoto effects; continuous movement of the element while shooting gives the characteristic zoom effect, closing in on or retreating from the subject being filmed.

Lenses are more accurately described by focal length – the distance from the centre of the main optical element of the lens to the plane of the film emulsion, most commonly expressed in millimetres, but often found marked in inches. On 16-mm. cameras, the standard focal length is 25 mm. or 1 inch. Lenses below this focal length are wide-angle: 16 mm. (0·7 in.) is frequently used, while 10 mm. and below are extreme wide-angle lenses, and may distort the image considerably. Of the long-focus and telephoto lenses, above 25 mm., 50 mm. (2 in.), 75 mm. (3 in.) and 100 mm. (4 in.) are commonly used, while lengths of up to 400 and 500 mm. are available. Zoom lenses vary widely in the range of focal lengths available: for example, the widely used Paillard Vario-Switar can give focal lengths ranging from 17 mm. to 85 mm., while Angenieux lenses, often used with Arriflex cameras, offer ranges from 12 mm. to 120 mm. or 12 mm. to 240 mm. Zoom lenses are sometimes described by the ratio of the longest focal length to the shortest, e.g. the Angenieux lenses referred to are often called 10:1 or 20:1 zooms.

Since various focal lengths produce special characteristics in the lenses, and since these characteristics have considerable bearing on the effect of the photographic image produced, the use of various types of lenses is discussed in Chapter 9.

The various types of movie camera available may have several from a range of other features, though few cameras will have them all. A lens turret, which accepts two or three lenses and enables them to be rotated in front of the shutter, facilitating a rapid change of lens without removing them from the camera, is found on most 16-mm. cameras. A matte box – usually a form of bellows attached to the front of the camera, with slots to hold filters, mattes (masks) etc. – is used most frequently with reflex cameras, since alignment of the camera through non-reflex viewfinders can be difficult with a matte box attached. On cameras required for live sound filming, whether sync or wild, a blimp (an enclosing sound-proof cover) is placed over the camera to prevent the sound of the camera motor from reaching the sound recorder. Some cameras, such as the Arriflex BL, are self-blimped, and an additional cover is not required. Many cameras are provided with a film magazine to take the film supply and take-up; the previously loaded magazine can be quickly attached to the camera, and sizes taking up to several hundred feet of film are obtainable. Frame counters are often featured in addition to the regular footage counter, permitting precise measurement of film shot, essential when fades or dissolves are to be produced in camera. Devices for producing automatic fades are available on cameras with variable shutters; filter slots may be built into the camera body, avoiding the need to attach a separate filter to each lens; extension tubes will enable extreme close-up work to be carried out; tachometers provide means of checking motor speed exactly. Other refinements of varying degrees of importance will be encountered on various cameras.

Whichever camera is used, it is important that the operator be fully acquainted with it. Many of the rules of camera operation are logical extensions of the mechanical workings of the camera, and good camerawork depends on being aware of all aspects of the camera itself, and the possibilities offered by it. Further, a thorough understanding of the camera leads to good camera maintenance, and an early awareness of any irregularity. The importance of good camera maintenance cannot be too heavily stressed: to ignore signs of fall-off in performance or of faulty mechanical operation can easily lead to the wastage of hundreds of feet of possibly irreplaceable film. The cost of re-shooting needlessly wasted film can be significant on a small budget, and in any case will probably be greater than the cost of a repair to a quickly detected fault.

Tripods. For by far the greater part of all camera-work, the camera will be mounted on some form of support, which not only takes the weight of the camera, but also

Arriflex tripod in use; for all normal shooting, a good tripod is essential.

ensures that all pictures turn out steady, and that all movements are smooth. The hand-held camera is frequently used, but on the whole for special purposes; for all normal shooting, the use of a good tripod is essential. Tripods vary enormously in design and detail, and it is most important to have one that is strong enough for the job, and one that enables smooth movements to be made.

The standard tripod is usually about 3 to 4 ft high with its legs in the closed position, but may be raised to perhaps 6 or 7 ft with its telescopic legs extended. For camera angles lower than are possible on a standard tripod, there are shorter versions available – a 'baby-legs' may range from a few inches to a couple of feet, while a 'hi-hat' (or 'top-hat') is a mount that rests directly on the floor, and enables very low angles to be taken. A hi-hat can also be placed on a table or other surface to make a camera support in places where a tripod could not be erected. Many tripods, whatever the length of their legs, will require a 'spreader' (or 'spider') – three slotted strips of metal, joined to a centre, which accept the feet of the tripod – to prevent the legs of the tripod from slipping apart when placed on hard or slippery surfaces.

The most important part of the tripod is the head, to which the camera is directly mounted. A good head should be provided with both a levelling device – preferably incorporating a spirit level, so that the camera can be set absolutely level without the tripod needing to be continually adjusted – and a 'fluid action', in which the movements are made against resistance from a viscous fluid held inside the head mechanism. This ensures that minor jerks and vibrations from the movement are smoothed out before reaching the camera, and that all movements are perfectly smooth. Other friction devices which have the same damping effect on unsteadiness are also incorporated in some tripods. Most sophisticated of all, perhaps, are the fairly recently developed gyro heads, which incorporate a gyroscopic mechanism and give rock-steady pictures and movements, even under otherwise alarming conditions. Otherwise, 'Moy' heads, whose movements are operated by gear movements controlled by rotating handles, are very widely used by well-equipped units, though they are often beyond the means of the small 16-mm. film units except for occasional hire.

At the other extreme, there are minimal camera supports for use when there is no time or space to erect a proper tripod, and for aiding hand-held camerawork. 'Shoulder pods' (illus., p. 76) or body harnesses are virtually indispensable for hand-holding the heavier 16-mm. camera, such as the Arriflex and the Eclair; with lighter cameras, a monopod – a single-leg support – or a pistol grip can be useful. Under all conditions, the maximum support available should be given to the camera while shooting.

Finally, tripods can often be mounted on or incorporated into mobile camera dollies and cranes. These are described in Chapter 8.

Film for tungsten light, 3200°K: exposed under correct light.

Film for daylight, 5000°K: exposed under correct light.

Film for tungsten light, 3200°K: exposed in daylight.

Film for daylight, 5000°K: exposed under 3200°K tungsten light.

Film for tungsten light, 3200°K: exposed in daylight with 85 filter.

Film for daylight, 5000°K: exposed under tungsten light with 80A filter.

FORCING EASTMANCOLOR
7254 FILM (16-MM. FRAME
ENLARGEMENT)

Exposed at normal rating (ASA 100).

Forced one stop (ASA 200).

Forced two stops (ASA 400).

4 Filmstocks

As with the mechanical workings of the camera, so is the understanding of the properties of filmstocks essential to good camerawork: a good working relationship with a filmstock or range of filmstocks is as important as knowing a particular camera well. Different filmstocks, together with the ways they are processed, can give different renderings of the same image, and as with all areas of cinematography, control of these variables is an important aspect of style.

16-mm. movie film is normally supplied on daylight loading spools of 50 or 100 ft, or on cores for loading into magazines, often of 400 ft, but ranging from 200 ft up to 1,000 ft. The film is perforated either down both sides (double perf.) or on either of the sides (single perf.), depending on the disposition of the feed sprockets in the camera to be used. With the 'winding A' the sprocket holes are on the near side of the film to the operator when the camera is being loaded: with 'winding B' the holes are on the far side. In either winding, the emulsion may be either facing in or out as the film comes off the reel, again to allow for different camera layouts. By far the most frequently used disposition is the 'winding B, emulsion-in' format, although, of course, double perf. film can be used with cameras with one set of drive sprockets, on either side, as well as with the few older or specialized cameras that have two sets of drive sprockets.

All filmstocks are coated on a cellulose acetate 'safety' base. The variable element in filmstocks is, of course, the emulsion – the light-sensitive layer that, when exposed and processed, will become the photographic image.

Different emulsions require different lengths of time to register the image presented to them by light focused through the lens. This variation in time required is described by the speed rating of the film, which is calibrated on one of several scales. The American Standards Association (ASA) scale of emulsion rating is most widely used in England and the USA; in Europe the Deutsche Industrie Norm (DIN) system predominates, and DIN ratings are usually given in addition to ASA ratings for filmstocks sold in England, while in Eastern Europe and the USSR the Russian GOST system is used. Other scales are found, including British Standard Arithmetic and Logarithmic (BS Arith. and BS Log.), Weston, and Hurther and Driffield (H & D), though these are either obsolete or rare. ASA is an arithmetical scale – the higher the ASA number the faster the film: i.e. a film of nominal rating ASA 250 will be twice the speed (needing half the exposure time or half

A winding

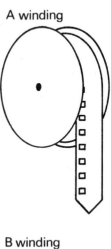

B winding

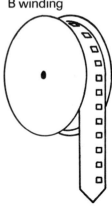

the aperture setting) of a film rated ASA 125, and half the speed (needing twice the exposure time or twice the aperture setting) of a film rated ASA 500. DIN is a logarithmic scale: to double a DIN rating, three units are added to the rating, and to halve the rating three units are subtracted. Thus 25 DIN equals twice 22 DIN and half 28 DIN. (25 DIN = 250 ASA.)

Most films are packed with a recommended speed rating marked on the box or can, and this, together with the recommended processing, should give optimum results. However, if consistently unsatisfactory results are obtained by using this rating, it is often advisable to adjust the recommended rating either up or down, until a rating suiting the individual operator is arrived at. The need for adjustment to rating may arise, for instance, if calibrations on equipment are slightly inaccurate, or if the operator's system of light assessment produces consistently undesirable exposures. There are many different ways of deciding which aperture to use, and it may be found that some do not give best results when the manufacturer's recommended rating is used for the filmstock. Temporary adjustment to speed ratings may be desirable under special lighting conditions, or for certain subjects. Speed rating for a film is usually lower for work under artificial illuminants than its rating for daylight exposure, but this is normally indicated on the film's data sheet and/or packing.

With certain filmstocks the recommended rating can be drastically changed to cope with extreme lighting conditions, usually a significant raising of the rating to compensate for low light levels. This is known as uprating or forcing, and may allow good pictures to be taken under light conditions where the film would not otherwise register a satisfactory image. When using a forced rating, the operator calculates his exposure on the basis of the desired speed index, and the film is clearly marked with this rating when it is sent to the labs for processing. The underexposure resulting from the higher rating is then compensated for by special extended processing techniques which bring the image up to the desired level. Forcing, however, produces a progressive increase in grain size: the more a film is forced, the grainier will be the image, and, where picture quality is important, film should not be forced unless this is unavoidable. Also, the more a film is forced, the greater becomes its contrast: extreme forcing may have the effect of knocking out many mid-tones. Further, with colour films, colour rendering is affected by forcing, and the cameraman must be prepared to accept appreciable loss of picture quality if he forces colour stocks to any great extent (see p. 34).

It is normally convenient to uprate films in terms of full stops of the camera lens: in other words, since doubling of film speed corresponds to an extra stop exposure through the lens, a film that is forced to twice its normal rating may be said to be forced by one stop. And because the stops increase in geometric progression, a film that is forced by two stops must be given four times the recommended rating. Thus, starting with a recommended rating of ASA 125, forcing by one stop produces an effective speed of ASA 250, and forcing by two stops, ASA 500. Forcing to over three stops (in this case 1,000 ASA) will be only used in emergency and with very few filmstocks, as at this stage picture quality may be very poor indeed. Some filmstocks are more suitable for forcing than others, and care should be taken that any forced footage is shot on a suitable stock. Ilford Mk V film, for instance, can be successfully forced to 1,000 and even possibly to 1,500 ASA, where Ilford FP4 should not be forced at all. Kodachrome II colour stock cannot be forced above its nominal rating, whereas Ektachrome Commercial 7252 can give reasonable results on one or even two stops above its recommended ASA 25. Knowledge of the filmstock is essential.

PROCESSING

Black-and-white film is processed in two ways: reversal, and negative/positive (usually abbreviated to neg./pos.). Each process is suited to particular uses, and the choice between them should be made before shooting starts, as intercutting between the two is undesirable. Reversal film, when processed, will be projected with the emulsion towards the gate of the projector ('emulsion-in'); while neg./pos., because the negative is printed on to a projecting print, with emulsion to emulsion in the printer, will have its emulsion away from the gate ('emulsion-out'). The thickness of the film base is sufficient to throw the projected image out of focus when the emulsion changes from one side of the base to the other, so either the reversal or the neg./pos. must be reprinted to line up the emulsion with the rest of the film. Apart from involving extra cost and time, reprinting will involve a loss of picture quality, which will be noticeable when reprinted material is projected intercut with original master. Tonal qualities and definition of the image will also vary, producing lapses in visual continuity.

In the neg./pos. process, the camera master film is developed as negative, and a print, which can be for cutting, duplicating or projection, is taken from it. This process has several advantages over reversal when a number of prints are required. The initial processing costs are lower, since reversal processing, which is lengthier than negative developing, is not required; and the cost of all subsequent prints is lower as, again, reversal processing is not needed. Hand processing for short lengths of film, or when maximum promptness is necessary, is far less complicated than reversal, and more control is available in developing. Photographically, there is more exposure latitude in negative stocks, making it easier to rescue poorly exposed material than in the case of reversal.

Also, the basic recommended speed rating of a filmstock is always higher when used negative than when used reversal, e.g. Kodak Four-X neg. is rated ASA 400 (ASA 320 in tungsten light), while Four-X reversal is rated ASA 200 (ASA 160 in tungsten light).

The chief drawback of the neg./pos. system, apart from slight additional complications in the final assembly of the master for printing, is where one projection copy only is needed quickly, when reversal is more suitable, and cheaper.

The big advantage of reversal stocks is the immediate availability of a projection copy from a single processing – one reversal master is cheaper than the combined developing and printing costs of neg./pos. However, because the reversal camera stock is master material, which ideally should never be projected or cut, the use of such single master reversal copies is limited mainly to amateurs. Reversal film is, however, frequently used as master material from which prints are taken, and has some advantages in this respect. Because the master image is positive, master assembly is quicker and easier; and where a great number of prints are required, an intermediate printing negative ('interneg.'), necessary to prevent excessive wear on the original master, can be taken as a direct print from the reversal master, thus avoiding reversal processing. So for great numbers of prints a reversal master may be slightly cheaper. Cutting-copies and small numbers of prints will still be dearer.

The photographic disadvantages of reversal include the added complexity of processing, the loss of exposure latitude, and the reduction in film speed, though none of these should necessarily present any great problem to a competent cameraman. There is also one area where a reversal master is essential: where it is desired to superimpose white titles over the picture. With reversal stock, unexposed film processes as black: with negative, however, it processes clear. For superimposition the background must be opaque on the master in order that only the lettering area shall be exposed on the print film, the rest remaining unexposed to receive the picture on to which the title is superimposed. If white letters on a black ground are filmed on negative, all the background area is clear on the master, and on printing this means that this area on the print film will be fully exposed, and thus unable to accept the background picture. It follows that, with negative master, any superimposed titles must be black, and this is often not as suitable as white for main titles, captions and subtitles. It is essential to consider these requirements when selecting filmstock.

When exposing black-and-white filmstock it is better when using reversal stock to underexpose slightly in case of doubt, while in negative it is better to overexpose slightly. Overexposure on negative stock produces an overdense image which increased printer light in the final printing of the film can penetrate, producing an acceptable printed image: underexposure will result in a thin negative image, with little rendering of detail. These lost details can never be restored. With reversal stock, underexposure produces the denser image, and overexposure the thinner; so for printing from reversal master, detail can be rescued from the underexposed image, while detail is lost in overexposed parts. In an emergency, reversal stocks can be exposed and processed as negative, and negative as reversal. The operator must remember, however, to adapt the recommended speed rating to the new process – halving the nominal rating for negative to reversal, and doubling it for reversal to negative. As with all departures from normal usage of a filmstock, the adaptation should be very clearly marked on the box or can and report sheet when the film is sent for processing.

BLACK-AND-WHITE 16-MM.

Most of the 16-mm. black-and-white filmstocks in use in Britain are manufactured by Kodak Ltd, Ilford, and Agfa-Gevaert Ltd. The following are their most widely used stocks:

Kodak

Plus-X. Available as negative and reversal, although the reversal is no longer classed as a professional film. An excellent medium-speed (ASA 125 neg., ASA 60 rev., in daylight) film, giving fine grain and full tonal range, which makes an admirable general-purpose stock. *Tri-X.* Negative and reversal, though reversal no longer classed as professional. A high-speed film (ASA 400 neg., ASA 200 rev.), giving good results at rated speeds but not generally suitable for forcing. *Four-X.* Now replacing Tri-X as main Kodak high-speed stock, with the same recommended rating as Tri-X but with improved specification; more suitable for forced processing.

Ilford

Pan F. A very slow, fine-grain film for use where abundant lighting is available, for maximum picture quality. Rated as ASA 25 (ASA 20 tungsten); negative only. *FP3, FP4.* Negative only available, rated ASA 125; a good general-purpose medium-speed film with fine grain. *Mark V.* Negative only. Rated as ASA 250, but a remarkably versatile film, giving excellent results when forced as far as ASA 500, and still producing reasonable pictures right up to ASA 1,500. An excellent film for use where light levels are very low indeed, or to produce contrast in dull and flatly lit subjects.

There are also films available for special purposes, such as high-contrast stock for titling, grey-base low-contrast films for television use, and stocks for specialized use, such as aerial filming and high-speed microphotography. Other manufacturers, including Orwo, Agfa and Ferrania, also have filmstocks available in Britain, but these are not as yet widely used.

As the film speed increases, the size of the grains in the emulsion grows larger – i.e. the film becomes grainier, and definition decreases. Therefore, for general purposes, the slowest filmstock that will cope easily with the light levels available should be chosen. However, since lenses rarely give their best results when they are used at their widest apertures, and the small depth of field offered by wide-open lenses may not be suitable for the occasion, it is often better to choose a filmstock that will allow mid-range apertures to be used.

COLOUR 16-MM.

With colour filmstocks there are other important factors to consider which do not apply to black-and-white. First, the quality of the light illuminating the subject is described in terms of the 'colour temperature' of the light. The colour temperature of light is measured in degrees on the Kelvin scale (°K). Degrees Kelvin are the same as degrees centigrade, but the Kelvin scale starts with absolute zero (-273 °C), thus 0 °C $= 273$ °K. The colour temperature of light is reckoned by the number of degrees Kelvin required to heat a specified black body to such an extent that it emits light of the corresponding colour. Thus light at the red end of the spectrum will appear at lower temperatures than light at the blue end of the spectrum. Light with a high red/yellow content, such as from most artificial illuminants, will have a relatively low colour temperature: for example, studio incandescent light sources are normally rated at 3,200 °K, and photoflood light at 3,400 °K. Daylight and skylight, with a high blue content, will have a Kelvin rating of between 5,000° and 6,000°, and upwards to 20,000 °K.

Colour film emulsion is balanced to give good colour rendering under certain specified light sources, and use of a film balanced for one type of illuminant will result under another light source in gross distortions of colour. Movie films are supplied balanced for either 3,200 °K (artificial type) or 5,400 °K (daylight type). If colour film for artificial light is exposed in daylight, a pronounced blue cast will pervade the colour, while if daylight film is used under artificial light, the colours will be tinged with an unpleasant yellow-ochre cast. Colour films can be adapted for use under incorrect light sources by colour correction filters. The exact filters recommended can be found in the data sheet supplied by the film's manufacturer: for example, a blue filter such as Kodak Wratten 80B may be used to enable a daylight-balanced film to be exposed under artificial light, and a pale amber filter, such as Kodak Wratten 85, will allow exposure of 3,200 °K film in daylight. But, wherever possible, the correctly balanced film should be used: conversion from artificial light to daylight is usually satisfactory, but the reverse is not always successful.

Second, the brightness ratio that colour films can accept is considerably less than that suitable for black-and-white emulsions. The brightness ratio of a scene is measured by the relation of the intensity of the light of the brightest area to that of the darkest. Whereas a black-and-white emulsion can accept brightness ratios of up to about 20:1 and still produce acceptable photographic images, a brightness ratio of 8:1 may be too much for a colour emulsion to cope with without colour distortion, or over- or underexposure on either the brightest, or the darkest, part of the scene. Lighting must, therefore, be carefully regulated to give a brightness ratio acceptable to the emulsion used; frequently, especially with uncontrolled light sources, where the brightness ratio is unavoidably too great for the emulsion to record all details faithfully, some compromise will have to be made in the exposure, allowing over- or underexposure in unimportant areas of the scene.

Exposure generally must be very carefully calculated with colour film: the margin of error is very small. With black-and-white film, errors of up to one or two stops may still produce quite acceptable pictures: with colour, errors of more than one-third, or at the most a half, of a stop may result in a significant loss of picture quality.

Third, most colour camera stocks have associated printing stocks, and are balanced to give best colour rendering on that printing stock. Kodak Ektachrome 7252, for instance, gives a rather soft rendering of colours, making it suitable for printing on to its associated Kodachrome printing stock, which restores the correct contrast to the colours. This must be borne in mind when ordering the final print.

Fourth, since different emulsions give very different renderings of colour, it is important not to mix different filmstocks, particularly within a scene, where colour continuity is as important as any other kind of continuity. Even films with names as similar as Ektachrome 7252 and Ektachrome 7242 should not be intercut.

Finally, colour master, even though reversal, should never be projected. Ideally, black-and-white reversal master should also not be projected, but colour emulsions are sometimes physically very soft, and are more prone than black-and-white master to damage in the projector or editing-machine. A possible exception to this is Kodachrome II camera reversal stock, which has a physically hard emulsion, and is not suitable for printing from in any case. This film is intended as a projection master, and is mainly used in the amateur market.

Colour processing is a more specialized procedure than black-and-white processing, and some colour films can only be processed by certain laboratories. Many labs can now process Kodak Ektachrome films, for example, but Kodachrome processing can only be done in the Kodak processing laboratories: remember this when ordering Kodachrome prints or Kodachrome II reversal processing. Some labs, furthermore, subcontract colour processing: additional delay in colour work may be expected here.

Working with a colour reversal master has advantages over colour negative. Some users prefer the colour quality of some reversal stocks to that of the few available negative stocks and, as with black-and-white, a positive image is easier to handle when assembling master material. Further, since colour quality can be assessed on the master, provided due care is taken, a black-and-white cutting-copy will suffice for the workprint, so saving the cost of a colour cutting-copy, which is really necessary from negative – though labs can supply colour pilots (short samples of printed footage) to go with a black-and-white cutting-copy.

When ordering black-and-white cutting-copies from colour master, specify whether they are to be printed on blue-sensitive stock, which is cheaper, but may not reproduce edge-fogging and other imperfections in the master, or on panchromatic stock, which will record all details.

Kodak colour films are by far the most widely used in 16-mm. film production, but Agfa's Gevachrome is becoming more widely available.

Kodak

Kodachrome II. A camera reversal projection stock, rated at ASA 25 daylight, ASA 40 photoflood, and available balanced either for daylight or photoflood illumination – type A for photoflood, type B for daylight.

It is not suitable for use as a printing master, and should not be forced. It has an anti-abrasion backing and a physically hard emulsion, and stands up well to projection. Suitable for use where no prints are required. It must be sent to Kodak labs for processing, and this can often take time. Its colour rendering is fairly hard, with strong contrast and vivid hues.

Ektachrome Commercial 7252. This stock is the direct successor of Ektachrome Commercial 7255, which for some time has been a standard and widely used colour camera stock for 16-mm. It is only available balanced for illumination of 3,200 °K, but can be converted to daylight use with Kodak Wratten filter No. 85, which reduces its speed by one-half. Its recommended rating is ASA 25, but it can be forced to ASA 50 with good results, and in emergency can be used up to ASA 100. It offers a full tonal range and pleasing colour rendering, and is designed to be printed on to Kodachrome printing stock; this increases the contrast from the master image, which is fairly soft. The emulsion is physically very soft, and should on no account be projected, as it is very liable to be damaged. Black-and-white cutting-copies are readily available, and most labs can supply Ektachrome cutting-copies quickly. It is an excellent all-round colour stock where adequate light levels are obtainable. *Ektachrome*

EF 7241 (daylight) and 7242 (3,200 °K) have been developed for use in colour television work, where shooting colour film under adverse lighting conditions is frequently necessary. EF 7241 is rated ASA 160, 7242 at ASA 125, but both produce good results when forced by one or even two stops, though colour rendering naturally suffers when up-rating by large amounts. The film is physically strong, and can be used as a reversal projection master, although an associated printing stock is now available. Most labs equipped for colour can process this stock. Colour rendering is very good, though it has a fairly soft contrast, to make it suitable for television transmission. It should not be intercut with Ektachrome 7255. *Eastmancolor 7251* is a high-speed colour negative stock which has rapidly gained favour over the last couple of years. It offers excellent colour renderings coupled with high ASA rating – normal is ASA 100, at which speed the picture quality is very good indeed. It can be forced comfortably to ASA 200, which allows much available-light night-time filming; and in emergencies can be used at ASA 400, although at this speed grain is noticeable, and colours tend to polarize towards the extremes. Being a negative stock, 7251 has good exposure latitude, and modern printing techniques make it possible to correct quite serious errors in the negative. Some labs are able to produce good colour quality even from 7254 shot in daylight without the appropriate filter. The illustrations on p. 33 show the range of colour correction that is available on printing from Eastmancolor negative. It is normally printed on to Eastmancolor 7381 printing stock.

Agfa-Gevaert

Gevachrome 6.00 is a medium-speed colour reversal stock, rated ASA 50, producing a sharp image and giving fine grain. Has a softish contrast, and can be printed on to Gevacolor. 9.85 (which has superseded the old type 9.02) to give high-quality projection prints. *Gevachrome 6·05* is a high-speed reversal colour stock, rated ASA 125, which retains a reasonable fineness of grain in relation to its speed, and can still be used for printing from, on 9.85. These two Gevachrome stocks can be processed in many labs, and are gradually gaining popularity as stocks comparable with Kodak 7252 and 7242. The Gevacolor printing stock, however, has an advantage over Kodachrome print stocks in that it can be processed by a number of different labs, whereas Kodachrome can only be processed by Kodak.

Colour rendering is very difficult to describe in words, and all cameramen have their own views as to the performance of the various filmstocks. The final choice of film must be made after experience with the various emulsions, and experimenting with their potentialities. Intimate knowledge of the filmstock and what it will do under varying conditions is of great importance in successful colour cinematography.

5 Lighting

Lighting is a virtually essential part of good ciné photography indoors and in the studio, and, under certain conditions, outdoors. It is a large subject which cannot be dealt with easily in a short space: there are many sound books devoted entirely to lighting, and the following is no more than a guide to the main points to bear in mind as awareness of lighting and its problems grows. The lighting of a scene has a crucial effect on the visual presentation of the completed film, and as such can be one of the major creative contributions to it. As with other creative aspects of the film, lighting depends to a large extent on the imagination of the man in charge: though the basic rules of lighting can be suggested, imagination cannot be taught.

The most obvious function of lighting is to provide enough illumination to allow a satisfactory exposure to be made on the chosen filmstock. Many colour films, and some black-and-white, can be exposed without artificial lighting only in conditions of reasonably bright sunshine exteriors; for all interior work with such stocks, good lighting will be essential to achieving good exposures. Many faster films, however, will allow exposures to be made in average indoor conditions: indeed, by forcing, some filmstocks could be made to produce pictures under almost any conditions bar total darkness.

Artificial lighting is, however, used for the majority of all indoor and studio work. It has the great advantage of allowing a very high degree of control over the appearance of the photographic image. In the first place, it allows the cameraman to choose whatever kind of filmstock he wishes: if he requires very fine grain and maximum sharpness, he can choose a very slow film and use plenty of lighting. If he needs a noticeable grain and high contrast, he may select a high-speed filmstock and reduce the lighting level, or stop his lens down. Even the slowest of colour stocks can be used, without forcing, to ensure good colour rendering. Artificial lighting provides pictures of good contrast, which is often lacking in general interior camerawork with natural light, where light sources are of low intensity, or are generally indeterminate. Lighting can be used to accentuate form, or to improve tone, or to level out or exaggerate tonal differences, according to the cameraman's need. Or the structure of the lighting may be used to direct attention to certain important details in the image. And so forth – the possibilities are enormous.

The art of successful lighting lies in developing a sense of knowing where, and why, out of all the possible positions (for, in theory, lights can be placed virtually anywhere, so long as they are out of the camera's field of view, and provide enough illumination for the exposure), the available lights should be placed to give the best effect. Best effect: because as with so much in cinematography there is no right, and no wrong. The final choice is one of a series of decisions that go together to make an individual style. There are, however, certain principles that have evolved about lighting, and certain types of light-sources that have proved most useful.

There are two main categories of lights: floodlights and spotlights. Floods provide a wide angle of over-all illumination for raising the general level of lighting, while spots provide small areas of concentrated light for more intense illumination of restricted areas; many lighting set-ups comprise both types. Skypan, Scoop and similar studio floods are single-reflector, high-power floodlights; but floodlighting, especially for background and soft over-all lighting, is often achieved by the use of a bank or trough consisting of several smaller reflectors grouped together to form a unit. Such compound units often have a diffuser fitted over them, to ensure that the light is soft and even. Spotlights, such as Pups and Inkie Dinkies, can often be focused, from a small intense beam to a fairly broad beam that can even serve as a small flood.

Quartz iodine and tungsten halogen lights are becoming increasingly popular as light sources in studio lampheads: these now offer high light output with compact size and long life, and are much more versatile than older forms of lighting. The high power and compactness of quartz iodine has also made practicable very small hand-held lighting units – Bar Lights and Sun-Guns – which can provide up to 30 minutes of light from easily portable batteries, and which are widely used in reportage and other fields, where speed and manoeuvrability are of prime importance.

(*Below*, *left*) Floodlight; (*below*) 250W Inkie Dinkie and 500W Pup.

Quartz-iodine lampheads.

The Colortran system of lighting has now become a standard feature of small-unit lighting equipment. This system is run from one converter which supplies up to five or six separate lampheads, and offers accurately metered control of the colour temperature of each light source. A variety of lampheads is available for use with the Colortran converter, ranging from the powerful 'Super 80' flood, giving 1,500W output, to the 500W 'Ciné King', which is available in spot or flood settings. The Colortran system is excellent for small-unit location work on account of its compactness and ease of transportation. Complete lighting set-ups for much general-purpose 16-mm. location filming can be packed into a normal-sized travelling-trunk.

A range of standard accessories is used with artificial lighting, giving extra control over quality and temperature of the light provided, and the area over which the light is directed. 'Barndoors' are adjustable flaps attached to the lamphead, which enable the operator to cut off the light beam at the bottom, top or either side of its area, and so to determine accurately the bounds of the area of illumination. A 'snoot' is a conical attachment which fits over the lens of the light, directing it into a small circular area. Diffuser-screens can either be attached directly to the lamphead, or placed in front of the light source on their own stands, to diffuse the concentrated light of the lamp. Apart from the standard range of tripods, supports for lampheads include: G-clamps, to fix lamps to any existing support; booms, to

(Left) Colortran set-up with one 'Super 80', two 'Ciné Kings' and one 'Super Kicker'; *(below)* the Colortran converter.

46

'Super 80' (*left*) and 'Ciné King' with blues fitted.

carry lights into areas where other support is impracticable; and 'Polecats', which fit tight between any parallel surfaces – e.g. walls or floor and ceiling – and bear lampheads on G-clamps.

Shooting in colour in conditions that necessitate a mixing of natural light and artificial light will normally create a discrepancy between the colour temperatures of the two sources, and this will affect the colour rendering of a filmstock balanced for either one or the other. In these circumstances, filters must be used to balance one or other of the light sources, to ensure compatibility with the filmstock chosen. This can be done either by placing amber gelatine filters ('gels') over windows and other sources of natural light (so correcting the daylight to the same temperature as the artificial illuminant), and using 3,200 °K film; or by placing blue filters ('blues') over the artificial lights to raise their colour temperature to the same level as that of daylight, when 5,400 °K film can be used. The problem of mixed light sources does not, of course, arise when using black-and-white film.

The position in which the lights are placed, and the lighting function they carry out, can loosely be described by the terms 'key light', 'fill light', 'rim light and back light', 'background light', and 'spot highlight'. Although these terms have general significance, it is misleading to think of them as precisely describing the functions of the lights, as in many cases the effects overlap, and in some cases only one or two lights will be in use. An understanding of the basic positions, however, will greatly assist in the initial layout of a lighting set-up: detailed adjustments can be made later to create the exact effect required.

The first light set is invariably the key light, or the modelling light, which provides the main illumination on the subject of the scene. It is often used as the reference point for the calculation of the exposure: the light reading is taken from areas illuminated by the key light, and the level of other lighting in the scene is brought up to this level.

The principle of key, fill and rim lighting.

High-key lighting: almost uniformly bright illumination.

The fill light, sometimes known as the main light, fills in broad areas that are left unlit by the key light, and softens any harsh shadows cast by it. The fill light is normally placed near the camera-subject axis, and is of a slightly lesser intensity than the key light. If light sources of similar intensity are used for both key and fill light, it may be necessary to move the fill light slightly further away from the subject than the key light. When moving light away from the subject, note that the intensity of the illumination provided falls off in an inverse square ratio to the lamp-to-subject distance: i.e. at twice a given lamp-to-subject distance, the intensity of illumination provided will be one-quarter, not one-half, of its original level.

The rim light or back light is placed facing towards the camera from a position behind the subject. It can be used to provide highlights on a limited area of the subject (e.g. on a person's hair), and can also serve to accent the outline of a subject placed against a background of similar tone. This last function is particularly useful in black-and-white filming: with colour film this difference is often marked by colour. Rim lighting without a key light can often be used to create a dramatic silhouette effect.

Background light is often provided by wide floods or banks of lights so placed as to bring up the lighting in the over-all composition to the level required to maintain a desirable brightness ratio. Spot highlights may be used as necessary to accentuate details. With black-and-white film particularly, brightly lit areas of the screen draw the eye powerfully, and their disposition can be of considerable importance both in composition and in editing.

Lighting set-ups fall broadly into two categories, determined according to the brightness ratio of the photographed image, and known as 'high-key' and 'low-key' set-ups

Low-key lighting: wide difference between brightest and darkest areas.

('key', as used here, should not be confused with 'key light'). In high-key lighting the illumination is almost uniformly bright, and has a very low brightness ratio, say 2:1, or 3:1. High-key lighting, which should never, of course, be confused with overexposure, is frequently used to enhance moods of cheerfulness, fantasy, gaiety, purity. Low-key lighting, which can be used to underline tension, drama, mystery, for example, occurs when a large brightness ratio is used, for instance, when one figure or face is lit in an otherwise black screen. In practice, of course, most lighting set-ups fall somewhere between the two extremes; a term such as 'middle key' or 'medium key' may be used, but defining lighting set-ups by their key is a relative, and fairly general classification. 'High key' is no more specific a term than is 'long-shot', nor is 'low key' more precise than 'close-up'.

Most of the above remarks apply equally well to lighting for still photography and for ciné: but lighting for ciné has several special problems. The essential difference is that with ciné photography movement is being lit and, as a subject moves, or as the camera moves, light relationships and intensities may vary. A figure walking about in a room, for instance, will need to be lit throughout its movements: moreover, the lighting must be arranged so that light levels do not fluctuate in a manner inconsistent with the apparent lighting suggested by the screen image. All shots containing movement must, therefore, be thoroughly rehearsed before the take; similarly when the camera is moved during the shot, care must be taken that the whole of the area appearing in the shot is lit in the appropriate manner.

Camera movements can also prevent certain placing of lights; a light used for a set-up might appear on screen, say, at the end of a panning shot. Cables, too, can easily be overlooked, and appear on the shot. A further danger from moving the camera is 'flare' – hexagonal patches of light appearing on the film – a result of stray light entering the lens directly from a light source: the danger is especially great from back lights. Reflections of lights in highly polished surfaces can also be overlooked: so, too, can shadows – not only marked multiple shadows of the subject, but also extraneous shadows of camera, crew and equipment. Again, rehearsal is necessary to ensure that all elements in the set-up are carefully controlled.

Continuity is as important in lighting as in any other area of cinematography. Lighting set-ups must be checked from shot to shot when interior shots are to be cut together, and lighting log-sheets are very useful in keeping detailed records of the set-ups used during the shooting of a scene, especially when there are likely to be breaks in the shooting. Rendering of colours evidently the same must be kept consistent from shot to shot, particularly in the case of flesh tones, which are likely to be a major focus of attention when the film is screened. As with other kinds of continuity, common sense and observation are vital. Other details to bear in mind include the treatment of on-screen light-sources – alterations in these (such as switching off a light) may have to be balanced by a comparable reduction in photographic lighting, although the use of photoflood bulbs in existing on-screen sockets may help in certain cases. Finally, the elements of composition dependent on lighting should be carefully analysed. The distribution of highlights may be important when the picture is cut, and the cameraman should try to leave the editor with a good cutting point. This can be provided, for example, by thoughtful lighting at the beginning and the end of the shot.

Exterior lighting is largely a question of accepting what light is available, and putting it to the best use. Artificial lighting on exteriors is sometimes used, particularly in large-unit professional film-making; but many smaller 16-mm. units will not have lighting of sufficient power to make this a regular feature. When filming in colour, and using artificial light mixed with daylight, take care always to balance the two kinds of light by use of filters and appropriate film-stocks, as when filming interiors with mixed lighting.

But even without artificial light sources, a certain amount can be done to use the available light to the best effect; and this depends to a large extent on developing an awareness of what the light actually is. For a start, the weather has a great effect on both the quality and the intensity of the light. Clear sky and strong sunlight will provide a strong illumination and high colour temperature, but will cause a high brightness ratio, and give strong contrast; whereas a cloudy bright day may provide equally strong illumination, and possibly equally high colour temperature, but will give an evenly distributed, softer light – the thin layer of cloud acting as a diffusing screen over the sun's light-source. These

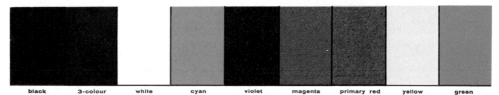

| black | 3-colour | white | cyan | violet | magenta | primary red | yellow | green |

B.S. 3020 Four-colour Inks

Kodak COLOUR PATCHES

Kodak GREY SCALE

C	Red-Filter Negative Cyan Printer		M	Green-Filter Negative Magenta Printer		Y	Blue-Filter Negative Yellow Printer	
0.00 A	0.10	0.20	0.30	0.50	0.70 M	1.00	1.30	1.60 B	1.90

Kodak colour patches and grey scale. These are exposed for a foot or two at the beginning of each roll of colour and black-and-white film respectively, and are used by the labs as a known reference scale when setting printer lights.

Control in colour printing (see p. 144). This frame enlargement from 16-mm. Eastmancolor film has been given correct balance by the printer light. The six illustrations overleaf show the wide variation of printer light balance, and thus the high degree of control over colour, that is possible in the printing process.

Variations on a frame (see preceding page). On most modern printers,
light balance is controlled by punched tape.

conditions may produce better pictures, especially on colour film, for the brightness ratio of subjects will be considerably reduced, and a better range of colour renderings result. Cloudy, dull or rainy days, however, may provide a light giving too little contrast, and produce flat pictures.

The weather must be assessed in relation to the kind of photographic effect it is likely to produce, and a decision taken as to the acceptability of the probable results. Different filmstocks will vary the effect of the prevailing light, and filters can be used to alter the photographic image. And the prevailing light itself can of course be slightly modified: artificial sources, properly balanced, can be used; reflectors made from white boards, or even a newspaper in emergency, are often useful for throwing light into dark corners. Choose the camera angle to make best use of natural reflectors, such as white walls. Reflectors, used in an imaginative way, can be a major or even exclusive source of light in difficult conditions. On one occasion, the interior of a Mycenean beehive tomb was lit to a level sufficient for Eastmancolor shooting by bouncing sunlight off a battery of reflectors outside on to another battery inside. Intelligent consideration of the use of reflectors can solve apparently difficult problems, especially in colour filming where mixed light sources may present difficulties in colour-temperature balance. If none of these adjustments to the lighting is successful, perhaps the shot could be lined up in a different way. With exteriors, the cameraman often has to adapt himself to the light, rather than adapting the light to his needs. Since natural light is present all the time, it is taken for granted, and developing an awareness of its effects needs a conscious effort. A panchromatic viewing glass or pan filter (p. 78) is a useful aid in assessing the effects of light, and should be kept with the camera accessories.

Whatever the lighting conditions, care and judgment must be exercised to use them to their best effect. Strong sunlight, which provides a strongly directional light (comparable with the effect of a key light in controlled artificial lighting), demands particular care: the pattern of shadows will be very evident on the screen, especially in colour film. The effect of shadows, for example, on the modelling of a face – or other essential contours of a subject – must be controlled to give the desired effect. Moving subjects present the same problems as under studio lighting – a clear example is afforded when a subject moves from bright sunlight into deep shadow. The low brightness ratio acceptable to most colour films will not allow a successful exposure in both sunlight and shadow areas, and some management of either the exposure or the light will be necessary. The exposure could be calculated as a mean between the two extremes, to give reasonable exposures in both areas, if the brightness ratio is not too great: otherwise the stop will have to be changed during the take. Either or both of these procedures may be unsatisfactory for the particular

Artificial exaggeration of lighting
effects: the shadows are painted on
the ground. (*Last Year in Marienbad*,
director Alain Resnais, 1962.)

Creation of visual texture by
elaborate lighting. (*The Scarlet
Empress*, director Josef von Sternberg,
1934.)

54

Use of natural lighting effect. (*Kes*, director Ken Loach, 1969.)

shot, and adjustment of the lighting may be tried, either by the addition of artificial light in the shadow areas, or by the use of reflectors. If neither of these alternatives is acceptable, the shot may have to be lined up from a different angle, or filmed in another place.

The angle of incidence of the light, particularly strong sunlight, is another critical factor in exterior lighting. The angles between the light-source and subject, and the subject and camera, provide a great range of alternative lighting effects; as with all aspects of lighting, these should be studied carefully. Possibilities of flat lighting, with the sun directly behind the camera (though the height of the sun should be noted), of side lighting, back lighting or rim lighting (complemented by artificial or reflected light at the front of the subject) present themselves; extreme effects such as *contre-jour* filming – directly against the light – and the deliberate use of flare can often be tried. Continuity for exterior lighting provides extra problems, particularly where there is strong sunlight. Since the sun shifts continuously, the angle of its strongly directional light will also shift: this can lead to problems of time continuity if an extended period is taken to shoot a scene of apparently short screen time. Such a scene may have to be shot on a series or one- or two-hour sessions on different days, rather than throughout one day. As with other continuity problems, observation and common sense are essential.

6 Exposure

Photographic exposure is an involved and technical subject to which many entire volumes have been devoted. What is offered here is merely a brief résumé of the basic facts needed in order to calculate reasonable general-purpose exposures; skill in judging exposures should be developed in conjunction with other aspects of camerawork.

Since movie film requires a given and constant amount of light falling on it to produce good photographic images, and since subjects filmed can vary enormously in the quantity of light they emit or reflect, the lens and shutter of the camera must be adjusted so that, whatever the brightness of the subject, the actual light reaching the film remains more or less constant. In a still camera, there are two means by which the amount of light transmitted by the lens can be adjusted: either the aperture of the lens can be opened or closed to let more or less light through at one shutter speed, or the time of opening of the shutter can be lengthened or shortened, to let more or less light through at one aperture. A number of factors affect the choice of combination of shutter speed and aperture.

In a ciné camera, however, since the film must move past the gate at a constant speed in order to reproduce a convincing effect of normal movement (except for slow- or fast-motion), there can only be one shutter speed – normally $\frac{1}{50}$ sec. at 24 f.p.s., $\frac{1}{30}$ sec. at 16 f.p.s. – and so adjustment can only be made by varying the aperture.

The aperture size is governed by an adjustable iris built into the lens, and operated by a ring built into the lens body. The size of the aperture is normally calibrated in 'f-stops', and the numbers of these stops are marked round the iris-adjusting ring. The f-number is calculated by dividing the focal length of the lens by the diameter of the aperture ($f = l/d$, where $l =$ focal length of lens, and $d =$ diameter of aperture),. and the conventionally used f-stops on modern cameras are 22 (the smallest aperture), 16, 11, 8, 5·6, 4, 2·8, 1·9. Intermediate f-stops on faster lenses often include 2, 1·8, 1·5, and, on slower lenses, 6·3, 4·3 and 3·5.

Each f-stop represents an aperture of double the area of the stop below it, and half the area of the stop above it, e.g. $f8 =$ twice the area of $f11$, but half the area of $f5·6$, and a quarter of the area of $f4$. In other words, the stops are arranged in a geometric progression.

The aperture must be opened and closed according to the amount of light available on the subject being filmed. For example, a very bright subject, such as an exterior in full sunshine, would need a small aperture – say $f22$; while an interior without special lighting, filmed on the same stock, would need a large aperture – perhaps $f1.9$. The exact setting is usually estimated with the aid of a light-meter (see below), since the amount of light available is often deceptive, even to an experienced eye.

The speed of the film is the other important factor in calculating exposure. Different films have emulsions which vary in their sensitivity to light, and thus in the amount of light they require to produce a good image. The aperture required to expose a given subject well will depend on the speed rating of the film: with a slow film of, say, ASA 25, an aperture of $f5.6$ may be necessary to expose a subject which would need an aperture of only $f16$ with a fast film of ASA 400. The choice of filmstock will often depend on the light levels expected at the location.

Accuracy of exposure is very important in cinemato-graphy. With still photography, much can be done in developing and printing to compensate for poor exposure, and many films have an 'exposure latitude' of several stops – a range of exposures within which it is possible to produce acceptable prints. The same is not true of movie films, especially for reversal stocks, where exposure should be accurate to about half a stop, or one stop at the most. A certain amount of printing-up can be effected at the labs, but this is relatively small; with reversal stocks, slight under-exposure is preferable to slight overexposure, while with negative stocks the reverse is the case. With colour films, nearly all of which are reversal in 16-mm., accurate exposure (to within one-third of a stop) is even more important. Inaccurate exposure of colour film not only renders the image too dark or too light, but also affects the colour rendering; and colour rendering must remain constant in a film.

The light-meter is an essential instrument in calculating the exposure. Light-meters vary considerably in design and in mode of operation, but all perform basically the same function of translating the intensity of the light falling on to their sensitive cell into figures; from these the operator can calculate, usually by scales on the meter itself, the amount of exposure necessary to produce a good result at the emulsion speed to which the meter is set. Instructions for the operation of individual light-meters are supplied with them when purchased.

Light-meters are generally used in one of two ways – for taking reflected light readings, or for taking incident light readings. For general use with ciné, for long shots, evenly illuminated scenes, and most exteriors, a reflected light reading will give a good idea of the light available. In reflected light readings, the light-sensitive cell of the meter is pointed towards the subject from the camera position, and the light reflected from the subject is measured. The exposure is then estimated from this reading.

An incident light reading is often useful for close-up filming, for animation and rostrum work, and for scenes of high brightness ratio. Whereas the reflected light reading measures the light reflected by the subject, the incident light reading responds to the light falling on the subject. A diffusing screen must be placed over the sensitive cell of the meter, to avoid distortion of the reading by bright highlights, and the cell, placed beside or in front of the subject, is then pointed towards the camera position. The meter takes into account all the light that falls on the subject from the direction it is being filmed from. The reading is taken, and the exposure calculated from it.

Some light-meters may not be equipped for taking incident light readings, however; or the nature of the subject may make it physically impossible. A method of adapting a reflected light reading for judging the average light reflectance of a subject with a large brightness range is the 'grey card' method. This involves placing a piece of neutral grey card, ideally of 18 per cent reflectance (special cards can be obtained for this), by the subject and taking a reflected light reading from this. An exposure calculated from this reading will indicate a good exposure for the average of the scene. If a grey card is not included in the camera equipment, the human hand makes a reasonable substitute for it. A reflected light reading from the hand – but make sure that the body does not cut off any of the light falling on the hand – will give a fairly accurate average exposure. A high brightness ratio may also be dealt with by averaging out the reading from the brightest area with that from the darkest.

Beware of large areas of brightness when taking an overall reading. The most frequent example of this is the influence of the sky in exteriors, or of large white backgrounds in interiors. When taking reflected light readings outside, be sure to point the meter slightly downwards, or the brightness from the sky will probably indicate a reading so high that you will underexpose your subject. This applies especially when a figure, for instance, is filmed against the sky. Unless you want a silhouette effect, take a reading close to the subject, and forget about the sky. It will be overexposed anyway, unless you are using special filters.

But whatever system is used, the operator must be careful to interpret and modify, if necessary, the indications of the light-meter. The meter can at best only tell what light is there, and recommend an all-purpose exposure. It cannot see the nature of the subject, and cannot make human judgments. For instance, in the case of extreme contrast, it may be desirable to keep the brighter part well exposed, and let the darker areas remain underexposed; or conversely, if the important action is taking place in a shadow area, it may be necessary to accept overexposure in a highlight in order to see what is going on where it really matters. In this, and in many other cases, the cameraman must use his judgment and experience in suiting his exposure to the particular circumstances. And it should be remembered that the light-meter is a tool to be used, not a god to be obeyed. It can often happen that an experienced cameraman will go against all advice from the light-meter when making his exposure calculations – and be right about it.

In cinematography, exposure must be consistent from one shot to the next. Variations in exposure are most noticeable on the screen, and while a certain amount of grading and colour correction is possible in the printing, to even out slight variations in exposure of the master, this can only be done to a limited extent before the printing-up or printing-down causes other inconsistencies in the photographic continuity of the film. Very great care should be taken with every exposure; where over-all consistency of exposure is impossible, try to be consistent at least with the main point of interest. For example, flesh tones – the human face, where used, will probably be a major centre of interest – must be kept consistent from shot to shot, even if this necessitates certain variations in the exposure of successive backgrounds. This principle should be adapted to fit most situations met in normal camerawork.

If a filter is used, be sure to compensate for the light it absorbs, when calculating the exposure. All filters have a 'filter factor' which indicates how much extra aperture should be given, expressed by a figure indicating the number of times the aperture area must be increased to transmit the equivalent amount of light. For example, a 'two times' ($2\times$) filter will need twice the aperture, i.e. one stop more than if no filter is in use; a $4\times$ filter will require two stops more, and an $8\times$ filter three stops more – since the stops progress geometrically.

The size of the lens aperture affects the depth of field of the lens, and so has very strong influence on the appearance of the photographic image. The depth of field is the distance between the nearest and furthest objects rendered in sharp focus by the lens, and it will primarily be affected by the focal length of the lens – the longer the focal length, the smaller the depth of field, other things being equal. But opening the aperture of any lens decreases the depth of field by considerable amounts.

The classic demonstration of this is to arrange a row of vertical objects – say candles – and place the camera looking up the line, about 10 or 20° out from the first candle, so that the candles are arranged in a receding line in the viewfinder. With the lens – a standard lens or longer should be used for the best effect – at maximum aperture (say $f1\cdot9$), focus it on

Effect of aperture on depth of field.

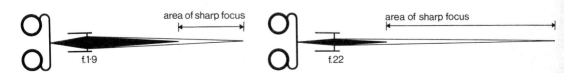

(Above, right) Full aperture; *(above)* stopped down to a small aperture, the camera can focus on the whole row.

the centre candle and take a picture. The aperture is then stopped right down, say to *f*22, and a further picture taken. When the two prints are compared it will be found that, in the first case, the centre candle only, and perhaps the two on either side of it, are in sharp focus. The second print, of the exposure made with the small aperture, will show most or all of the entire line in focus.

The depth-of-field factor is of considerable significance in camerawork, and the cameraman should be able to use varying depths of field at will. With the movie camera, though, it is not possible to compensate for different apertures by using different shutter speeds, as with still photography. The movie cameraman must, therefore, use other means to compensate for varying apertures, where this would normally produce unsatisfactory exposures. Firstly, he can select filmstock of a speed at which the apertures he envisages are suitable for the expected light situations, or he can alter the level of the lighting to suit his purposes. Secondly, he can use neutral density filters to cut down the amount of light reaching the film at a given aperture, allowing him to use one, two or more extra stops of his lens. Other filters may, of course, be used if additional effects are required.

Finally, remember that there is really no such thing as a 'correct' exposure. The lowest point at which a satisfactory image, recording all details and highlights, can be formed is known as the 'minimum correct exposure', and this is what is aimed for in calculating most everyday exposures. However, the balance of the exposure, the contrast and lighting, the special allowances for highlight and shadow, the depth of field, the atmosphere of the scene, photographic continuity and special photographic effects must all be borne in mind when calculating exposure. Exposure is in some measure a creative process – often calling for conscious choices between equally valid alternatives, and contributing materially to the visual structure and surface of the film – and requires judgment, imagination and, later, experience, in making the final decision as to the best exposure.

7 Camera operation

The operation of the camera is one of the routine tasks of film-making. Every camera has some features that are standard to all cameras, and some features that are peculiar to the particular model. The cameraman must be sure, before he starts filming that he is fully conversant with every detail of the camera; he should be so familiar with his camera that he can perform most of the operations and adjustments necessary without even having to remove his eye from the viewfinder; confidence in the operation of the camera is essential to good camerawork.

First, then, be sure that all details of the camera are understood: if you are using it for the first time, make a point of reading the handbook thoroughly, or of talking about the camera with someone fully experienced in its operation. Halfway through an irreplaceable shot is no time to find out that the variable shutter is in the closed position! Establish a pattern of working, and follow it always. There are a number of things to be constantly remembered and checked while filming, and the only sure way not to forget one or more of these is to establish a routine which includes them all, and stick to it. A basic camera drill, such as 'focus – aperture – motor' (FAM) will ensure that, provided initial checks have been carried out, the intended pictures are recorded every time. If the focus is correctly adjusted, the exposure reasonably accurately calculated and set, and the motor has sufficient drive to complete the shot, the cameraman can be certain that what he shoots will be satisfactorily recorded on the film, barring accidents at the labs.

FAM may be a useful drill to use between shots, but it can only be useful when it is used as part of a larger scheme which will include frequent checks on a much wider range of factors.

CLEANING AND LOADING

Camera loading systems vary between every type of camera – automatic or hand-threading, spool, cassette or magazine, daylight or darkroom loading – and the instructions in the camera's handbook must be exactly followed. Whatever the loading system, though, whatever the camera, the inside of the film chamber and the intermittent movement mechanism must be thoroughly cleaned. A blower brush, a selvyt cloth and, if necessary, a piece of soft wood, such as a toothpick, will be needed: see that they are included in the camera kit, and are on the camera checklist. The camera interior must be cleaned between every loading: the chief extraneous element which collects in a camera is emulsion particles scraped off the film as it passes through the gate and transport mechanism. Even the quantity of emulsion that collects during the shooting of 100 ft of film can lodge in the gate, and is sufficient to show up as a large black mark on the film when it is processed. And film ruined by a dirty gate cannot be rescued: the only answer is to reshoot, and clean the camera more thoroughly.

When the camera is loaded, check that the film is running correctly through the transport mechanism and gate before replacing the back of the camera: check that the back-plate is seated correctly and firmly secured. If the camera is magazine-loading, check that the magazine is properly seated and secured, and that the light-traps are perfect. All these operations must be done in subdued light – edge-fogging does occur if light conditions are not suitable.

PRE-SHOOTING CHECKS

Once the camera is loaded, secure it on its tripod and check that the motor is fully wound, if clockwork, or connected correctly to fully charged batteries, if electric. Set footage and frame-counters to zero (or to the pre-zero mark, if there is one), and run off the amount of film – usually five or six feet – provided on the front of the roll as integral leader, until the appropriate zero mark shows in the footage indicator. The running speed of the motor can be checked at the same time, especially with battery-driven cameras connected to freshly charged batteries, where the running speed may be much too high. Next, remove the lens caps, and open the variable shutter, if fitted, to the required angle of opening. If the viewfinder is of a non-reflex type, check that it is adjusted for the focal length of lens in use, and that any parallax error is compensated for. Ensure that the required lens is in the taking position, and that any filter required is attached to the lens, or placed in its slot or holder. Minor adjustments, and those peculiar to certain cameras, can now be carried out. These will vary considerably, but everything should be carefully checked.

Now focus the lens, calculate and set the best aperture for the light conditions, and the camera will be ready to shoot. Press the release button smoothly and firmly, and leave the camera running a second or two before the command 'action' is given: this will make sure that the motor is running to speed by the start of the take, and that 'flash-frames' (completely bleached-out frames which have been over-exposed before the motor has got to speed) are avoided during the actual take. An extra second or two may also help the editor by giving him room to put an emergency mix or fade on the beginning of the shot. At the end of the take, keep the camera running for an extra second or so, for the same reasons, and release the button smartly.

Immediately carry out any between-shot checks: focus and aperture will not be verifiable until the next camera set-up is decided, but any change of conditions or requirements can be dealt with at once. Most important of all is to check the motor after every shot: this should become habit. With clockwork motors, it is essential to wind the spring after every take, however short: cutting-room waste-bins are littered with shots that stop halfway through a vital movement. Besides, a fully wound motor means that the film transport is running as evenly as possible: even though clockwork camera motors have fairly accurate governors and cut-out systems, it very often happens that the last foot or two of a motor's run is slightly wayward. Electric motors, too, should be checked frequently, and batteries changed too early rather than too late.

Most important of all, it should be repeated, is to form a routine for carrying out these operations, and to stick to that routine under all circumstances. A successful cameraman uses the camera like an extension of his own body: the actual operation of it becomes a conditioned reflex, and his mind is left free to deal with the problems of what actually to record on the film.

SYNC SHOOTING

For shooting synchronous sound, all the above checks must be carried out on the camera, but in addition the sound recorder must be checked, and the links between camera and recorder; the correct procedure for marking the takes and starting the shooting of the takes must also be followed. Additional checks to be carried out before each sync take are: to ensure that sufficient tape is left in the recorder (remember that tape and film are used up at different rates); that all connections are correct and functioning; that the record level of the tape recorder is correctly adjusted (unless automatic, when its functioning should be tested); that the mike boom does not appear on the picture, even when the camera moves; that the clapper-board is clearly and correctly marked.

The clapper-board.

It is as well, wherever possible, to rehearse any camera movements thoroughly, especially those requiring the camera to move from one position to another – tracking shots etc. – in order to sort out boom movements, cable positions and suchlike. A movement rehearsal costs only a few minutes' time: a retake costs film and processing as well, and a large number of avoidable retakes can well upset a small budget. Further, new details will be continually observed during camera rehearsals and the best possible movement obtained in the actual take.

Camera crew: marking the slate.

The procedure for sync shooting is as follows:

1 Write the slate and take number on the clapper-board; have the clapper-board held in front of the camera, in a position where it can be clearly read through the view-finder.

2 Start the tape recorder running. When it is running to speed, the sound recordist should call, 'running'.

3 Start the camera running. After a second or two, when the motor is at speed, the mark should be made with the clapper-board: the clapper-board operator reads out clearly the slate and take number written on the board, and brings the clapper-arm down smartly on to the top of the board, making a distinct sound. The clapper-board should then be removed as quickly as possible. When it is well clear of the frame, there should be a further pause of a second or two before the call 'action' is given. At the end of the take, likewise, allow a second or two before switching the motor off.

Alternatively, the camera may be provided with an automatic marking device: a press-switch connected by a cable to the camera, which records a bleep on the sound tape, and at the same time fogs a few frames of film in the camera. The first frame of the fogging and the first frame of the bleep are then matched up instead of the respective 'strike frames' (see p. 118). Shooting procedure with the automatic marker is basically the same as with the clapper-board: the tape recorder is switched on, then the camera; the slate and take numbers are written on a card and held in front of the camera, and the announcement of the slate and take is made into the microphone: then, instead of the clapper being struck, the marker button is depressed for a brief moment. The end result is the same, but the automatic marking system has the advantage that it can be operated

Two-man sound and camera crew.

quite comfortably by two people, whereas the clapper-board system requires three.

All the time that shooting continues, the camera operator, or his assistant, should keep a camera report sheet in which he notes full technical details of every take. Specially prepared report forms can be obtained from labs and general film suppliers, and these should always be used. They should record details such as slate and take number, action, film-stock, location, interior/exterior, day/night, sync/mute, camera speed, aperture, camera number, and any other

Standard forms for picture (*left*) and sound reports.

LABORATORIES COPY   82652

CONTINUED FROM SHEET No.	SHEET NUMBER	CONTINUED ON SHEET No.

THE SHEET NUMBERS MUST BE QUOTED ON ALL DELIVERY NOTES, INVOICES AND OTHER COMMUNICATIONS RELATING THERETO

PRODUCING COMPANY _____ STUDIOS OR LOCATION _____

PRODUCTION _____ PRODUCTION No. _____

DIRECTOR _____ CAMERAMAN _____ DATE _____

STATE IF COLOUR OR B & W

PICTURE NEGATIVE REPORT

ORDER TO _____ LABORATORIES

STOCK AND CODE No. _____ LABORATORY INSTRUCTIONS RE INVOICING, DELIVERY, ETC. _____ CAMERA AND NUMBER

EMULSION AND ROLL No. _____ CAMERA OPERATOR

LENGTH LOADED	SLATE No.	TAKE No.	COUNTER READING	TAKE LENGTH	'V' FOR PRINT B & W COL'S	LENS F/L & STOP	ESSENTIAL INFORMATION see requirements below	CAN No.

	FOR OFFICE ONLY	TOTAL CANS

TOTAL EXPOSED		TOTAL PRINTED		TOTAL FOOTAGE PREVIOUSLY DRAWN	
HELD OR NOT SENT		B & W		FOOTAGE DRAWN TODAY	
TOTAL DEVELOPED		COLOUR		PREVIOUSLY EXPOSED	
				EXPOSED TODAY	

SIGNED : _____
COLOUR DESCRIPTION OF SCENE. FILTER AND/OR DIFFUSION USED DAY, NIGHT OR OTHER EFFECTS, DAYLIGHT, ARCS, INKIES OR MIXED LIGHTING.   INTERIOR/EXTERIOR A.M., P.M.

SAMUELSON FILM SERVICE LIMITED	303-305 CRICKLEWOOD BROADWAY EDGWARE ROAD LONDON, N.W.2 Telephone: GLAdstone 0123 Sound Dept.: Ext. 48/49	MAGNETIC SOUND REPORT										
ROLL No.:	SLATE	1	2	3	4	5	6	7	8	9	10	Source of Ref. Pulse and Remarks
PRODUCTION CO.												
PRODUCTION												
DIRECTOR												
MIXER												
JOB No.:												
RECORDER												
SPEED 3¾/7½/15" CCIR/NAB												
TRANSFER TO 16/17.5/35mm ¼" TAPE SPEED : 24/25 F.P.S. 50/60 CYCLES EDGE TRACK / CENTRE TRACK												
SEND RUSHES TO												

PRINT CIRCLED TAKES ONLY

relevant information. Which takes are worth printing, and which are not, may also be listed, especially on large-scale productions where many takes of each slate are shot. The sound recordist should also keep a sound report on similar lines, with details of all takes, plus general information about type of recorder, tape speed, sync system or wild, full or half track, date, production etc.

When shooting is finished, the film should be removed from the camera straightaway, and replaced in its original can. If for some reason the original can is not available, make sure that all misleading labels are removed from the can used, and that full details of the film inside are marked on the can. Film given the wrong processing will almost certainly be ruined. Seal the can with camera tape, and affix the relevant report sheet to the can, together with any special processing instructions – 'forced rating' or 'incomplete reel', for example. If the film in the camera has only been partly used – say 200 ft off a 400-ft core – the film may be 'short-ended' – the exposed part cut off and packed up for processing, and the short end returned to its packing unexposed. Again, clear marking is important: a cameraman on a subsequent session would be justifiably annoyed to find he had only 200 ft in a 400-ft can, and no warning.

In marking the can – and report sheet – for processing, it is most important to report any suspected damage to the film. If there is any likelihood at all of film having been torn in the camera, a clear warning – 'suspect torn perfs.', for example – *must* be sent with the film. One damaged length of film can cause a whole processing machine to break down: in that case all film in it at the time might well be lost.

Clearly packed and labelled film is then delivered to the labs, with instructions for processing, and for printing of rushes. The camera operator's last job is to dismantle and clean the equipment. When possible, this should be done methodically and carefully, with leads properly coiled and tied, and everything correctly stowed in its right case. Finally, run through the checklist and make sure nothing has been left behind.

8 Camerawork

Camera *operation*, as the last chapter has shown, is a technique which can be learnt simply and straightforwardly, and it must be mastered before the skills and complexities of *camerawork* can be attempted. Good camera operation is the 'bread and butter' of shooting any film: good camerawork is something more than that – it is crucial to the success of the film.

Camerawork is the translation of action into the screen image. It involves deciding what to record on the film with the camera. It is not primarily a narrative undertaking: after all, if a camera is just put in front of the subject of the film and set running, while the subject enacts the film's narrative content, the narrative will be recorded on film. But the odds are long against it being an interesting film rendering of the subject.

Film is the interaction between the recording medium (filmstock etc.) and the actions it is recording: the way in which the subject is recorded is as vital a part of the finished work as is the nature of the subject itself. For example, if the subject is a boy walking down the street, the filmic effect, and the impact on an audience, will be different if, say, he is filmed with the sun behind him, giving a back-lighting effect, or with the sun behind the camera, giving a harsh, fairly flat lighting. The effect if the background is kept in focus will differ from the effect if it is out of focus – the boy's relationship to his surroundings will have changed, in film terms, even though all details are otherwise precisely the same.

Many of the decisions as to the final visual interpretation of the subject will rest with the cameraman, though he will certainly be prompted by the director and by the script. Above all, the decision as to the framing of the shot – which is always crucial – will almost always be made by the cameraman. His skill and experience, and visual sensitivity, will be called upon for every shot. The cameraman's decisions at shooting are important throughout the film. Once the shot has been taken, the decision is finally made, and cannot be reversed. The film unit is stuck with the cameraman's decision of the moment: no chance of re-editing, as the editor can do if things go wrong; no chance of rewriting a passage, as when the script-writer sees his ideas going astray; no chance of a library sound effect to patch up a passage of poor recording. The cameraman's only let-out is re-shooting, and the possibilities of this are obviously very limited – by

finance, time, and availability of subject. So the cameraman must learn to see things as they will appear on the
screen, and to assess all alternatives in the short time he has
available for lining up the shot. Each shot and each movement should be rehearsed until the cameraman is sure that
they are right. He should be aiming to prevent the editor
from ever thinking: 'I wish he had taken this shot from
slightly further to the left . . .'. It is probably true that a
cameraman should have had some experience in picture
editing.

Although camerawork is chiefly dependent on creative
imagination and flair, there are a number of well-established
rules – perhaps guidelines would be a better term – of
camerawork which have grown up with the development
of cinematography. Although many of these will be frequently ignored by experienced cameramen, it is important
to know what they are, and why they came about. To ignore
through ignorance is rarely commendable, and analysing
the problems of camerawork is a valuable step towards the
understanding of the film form.

SHOT TYPES

The descriptive categories that shots are normally divided
into – long-shot (LS), medium-shot (MS) and close-up (CU) –
are no more than approximate guides to the general type of
shot: they have no specific meaning. These terms will differ
in their precise connotation from film to film and scene to
scene; a shot that merits the description LS by one film-
maker in a claustrophobic indoor scene may well be described as medium close-up in a wide open outdoor set.
These terms are merely convenient reference language
between the members of a particular unit: as long as everybody concerned understands the scale of reference, that is all
that matters. A fairly standard definition of the main shot
categories might be:

Long-Shot – any shot containing a full-length human figure,
   or capable of containing one; or any shot containing
   more than this.
Medium-Shot – containing between a full-length figure and
   a half-figure, or comparable subject size.
Close-Up – containing less than a half-length figure, or
   comparable subject size.

These definitions are arbitrary, but, once established, can be
modified to enable more accurate descriptions to be made:

ELS – Extreme Long-Shot (distant views etc.).
MLS – Medium Long-Shot.
MCU – Medium Close-Up.
CS – Close-Shot (sometimes used to signify a stage between
   MS and CU).

BCU – Big Close-Up (less than a whole face).
VBCU – Very Big Close-Up (an eye, or a pin-head filling the screen).

These terms, as well as even more elaborate ones, will be found widely used among film-makers. Once a standard for these terms has been set, it should be adhered to, however, for without it there can be no close communication between the director and cameraman, and, more important, the script-writer. The script-writer should define his terms in the script by describing in some detail just what he envisages on screen, until his terms of reference are apparent.

CAMERA MOVEMENTS

Camera movements are of two kinds – those where the camera moves on its mounting, and those in which the whole camera and mounting are moved bodily from one place to another. These two types of movement may also be combined.

Fixed-camera movements

The 'pan' (an abbreviation for panorama) is the horizontal rotation of the camera, moving on a fixed point, the tripod head. The pan is probably the most used of all camera movements; it is also one of the easiest to misuse, so any use of a panning shot should be carefully considered. First, never use a pan just to get the subject in. If a pan seems necessary, try either changing the camera position or using a wider-angle lens. The philosophy of 'plonk-the-camera-down-and-wave-it-around-until-we've-got-it-all-in' has no place in any kind of film-making, even the most rudimentary. However, certain subjects may benefit from being progressively revealed in a pan, perhaps even combined with a zoom-out, and in this case the cameraman's task is to find the best position for filming the pan from. Moving subjects will also often need a panning movement to keep them in frame for the duration of the shot. Broad, horizontal compositions may be improved by a panning movement; and some subjects – the countryside for example – may be too big to film successfully without panning.

If a pan is chosen, there are a few rules to consider. First, always begin and end the pan on a strong image. There is a saying that the bad cameraman 'pans from nowhere to damn-all', and it is salutary to recall this every time a pan is being set up. Really justify that pan. Secondly, hold the composition at the beginning of the pan and at the end of the pan for a few seconds: the editor will almost certainly use the held composition to steady the effect of the pan. If he does not require the held image, he can easily cut it off; he cannot add it if it is not there. Thirdly, the pan must be reasonably slow – unless a quick pan is specifically scripted – and, above all, smooth. A jerky pan is a nightmare. If the subject contains no movement, it is often a useful device to run the camera in slow motion (not forgetting to make necessary adjustments to exposure), in order to iron out the effect of slight tremors in the filming of the pan. This will also help compensate for the almost universal failing of inexperienced cameramen, that of panning too quickly. Apart from the unsettling effect on an audience of a pan that is too fast for the eye to follow comfortably, a fast pan will also have pronounced flicker, and this is physically uncomfortable to watch.

Above all, don't pan more than necessary in a film: the eye does tire of continual movement of this nature. More important still, do not 'reverse pan', i.e. follow one pan immediately with another in the opposite direction. This, however, is only little brother to the camera technique known as 'hosepiping' – where the camera is switched on and panned and tilted all over the subject, without a break. Everybody experiments with this technique once in their career: nobody does twice.

Panning is often necessary in order to follow a moving subject. When this is the case, there are several points to notice. At the beginning of the shot, let the subject move into a static composition, and at the end hold a static composition for the subject to move out of. This presents the editor with a number of alternatives to choose from when he is cutting the picture. Pick up the movement smoothly, and keep the moving subject in a constant position in the frame: preferably slightly to left of centre if movement is towards the right, and slightly to right of centre if movement is the other way. In other words, keep the frame slightly ahead of the subject, so that the subject is moving into the frame. Keeping the subject close to the side of the frame is also possible, providing it (or he) is moving into the frame; keeping it on the other edge of the frame is less conventional, and may prove unsuccessful unless there are particular stylistic demands. Finally, an almost universally regarded rule: do not pan against the direction of the main action of a shot. Apart from the fact that your shot probably won't last very long, panning against the movement increases flicker, and is generally rather disturbing to watch.

A variant on the pan is the special effect known as the zip-pan, whip-pan or blur-pan, which uses a pan so fast as to blur any details of the subject, and conceal a transition from one shot to another. This may be effected by splicing in a short length of zip-pan footage between two shots, or else by ending one shot with a very quick pan away from the subject, and joining it to another shot which starts with a rapid pan to the subject. Care should be taken to match the speeds of the two fast pans, or the change from one to the other will become apparent.

The tilt is the vertical equivalent of the pan, and in fact the up-and-down movement of the camera is often loosely referred to as a pan. All the same considerations as apply to

(*Above, left*) High angle (*Pharaoh*, director Jerzy Kawalerowicz, 1929); (*above*) low angle (*Strike*, director S. M. Eisenstein, 1924).

the pan apply to the tilt; one extra consideration to look out for when tilting is that, since the light from the sky is usually stronger than that from the ground, it is frequently necessary to open or close the aperture during the course of a tilt shot (see 'stop-pulling', below). When tilting, as with panning, take into account the distorting effect of lenses, particularly wide-angle lenses. As soon as the camera starts to move, the distortion is applied to the movement as well as to the form of the subject: this has a very marked effect, and unless specifically required, should be guarded against.

Mobile-camera movements

In the tracking or dolly shot the camera is moved in a horizontal plane towards, away from, or about the subject. This involves the use of a tripod mounted on a mobile platform, called a dolly, possibly running on some kind of temporarily laid track to keep the movement smooth – hence the name 'tracking' shot. Thus, the camera can move from long-shot to close-up (or vice versa) during the progress of the shot, producing the familiar effect so useful for pointing details, focusing attention on people or objects, relating subjects to their surroundings and many other purposes. Lateral tracking shots can be used to regroup compositions on screen, to give a variety of angles on the subject, or to film in one shot what might otherwise have needed several: shots with camera movement tend to conceal their actual length, and a shot which, if filmed static, would seem far too long, may well appear of the right length when a movement is included. Because something is always happening visually, camera movements distract the audience's attention from the actual duration of the shot. Tracking shots, like all other camera movements, must always be carried out as smoothly as possible.

Dollies are very varied in design, from complicated, motorized, steerable machines which carry the cameraman, an assistant and perhaps a sound recordist as well, to a simple home-made platform with fixed wheels and just enough room for a tripod and an operator. Where a proper dolly is

A simple location dolly.

not available, there is plenty of scope for improvisation. A wheel-chair, for example, bearing a cameraman and a hand-held camera, can be very effective; a moving car, also, is very useful, especially for high-speed exterior tracking shots. When filming from a car, better results will be obtained with hand-holding than with any form of rigid mount fixed to the car: the operator's body acts as a kind of shock-absorber, whereas a rigid mount transmits the full force of every jolt. Although shots taken from a car look very jerky through the viewfinder, in fact the speed of the movement compensates for the jolting of the camera, and the results are normally quite acceptable on screen.

The crane shot is the vertical equivalent of the tracking shot, where the camera is lifted or lowered by means of an elevating platform. Camera cranes, like dollies, vary from the large motorized versions, with hydraulic lifts and ranges of several metres of lift, and platforms for camera, operator and assistant, to small limited-lift cranes with short movements and mounting for the camera only. A velocilator is a kind of medium-sized mobile dolly with limited crane facilities, capable of carrying heavy cameras and an operator. By and large, extensive crane shots are beyond the scope of small film units, as suitable camera cranes are very expensive both to buy and hire. The adventurous cameraman, though, will be on the lookout for improvised crane shots, thumbing a ride on builders' elevators, fork-lift trucks, lamp-post maintenance lifts and so forth. Also, a limited crane effect can be got by hand-holding, with the cameraman raising himself from the squatting to the standing position – though this calls for great steadiness and balance to produce a picture steady enough to use. The occasional crane shot is well worth trying for: large-scale or unusual camera movements, always provided they are purposeful, can often provide considerable impact on the screen, particularly in small-scale films, where they are not taken for granted in the same way as in large-scale feature films.

The zoom shot is not strictly a camera movement, but because it has some superficial resemblance to the tracking shot, and can sometimes be used in the same circumstances, it is perhaps best discussed at this point. In the zoom shot the camera is static and the focal length of the lens is altered, giving the effect on screen of approaching towards or receding from the subject. This is very striking, but can all too easily be overdone by a too enthusiastic cameraman, especially as all different speeds of zoom are available at the operator's fingertip. Of all camera-movement effects, the zoom is probably the easiest to overwork and abuse: for this very reason it should be treated with caution, and only used when nothing else will do. On the whole, pulling back (zooming-out) is less blatant than zooming-in, and can also produce considerable dynamism, for, by starting on a detail, some sense of anticipation is inevitably created, especially if that detail is not immediately clear. To resolve this mystery by

Extreme wide-angle lens. (*Clockwork Orange*, director Stanley Kubrick, 1971.)

pulling back can be a very powerful camera device, but again, it must not be overdone. Almost invariably, the more powerful a cinematic device, the less frequently it should be employed, especially within one film.

The visual appearance of the zoom, although superficially similar to that of the tracking shot, is in fact considerably different, and the difference must be borne in mind when choosing between the two. The main difference is that with a tracking shot, the *actual* perspective of the subject changes as the camera moves; while with the zoom shot the *apparent* perspective shifts. This is noticeable as, in the case of the tracking shot, the spatial relationship between the main subject and his background changes, while in the zoom, the relationship stays the same: we see a smaller area of the total image, enlarged, and that is what makes it appear closer.

There are also further complexities: for example, other camera movements can be incorporated into a dolly shot, and the track need not continue in a straight line towards the close-up position: the track may, for example, start off by closing in on the subject, and then begin to circle it, viewing it from all sides.

When zooming, the focal length of the lens is constantly changing, and, with it, the characteristics of the lens, in the same measure; the difference of effect between an image shot on a wide-angle lens, and a section of the same image shot through a telephoto lens will show up. First, the effect of perspective is completely altered between the two extremes, from exaggerated perspective at the wide-angle end to flattened perspective at the telephoto. Secondly, the depth of field decreases as the focal length increases, and, especially at wide apertures, the depth of field may dwindle to almost nothing. This characteristic can have useful applications – such as singling out a man in a crowd, or a bird in a bush – but if the special effect is not required, it may militate against the use of the zoom.

73

Differential focus, to isolate one face.
(*Up the Junction*, director Peter
Collinson, 1968.)

It is worth remarking at this point that the zoom lens
should always be focused with its aperture fully open (as
should any lens), and at its longest focal length, whatever
focal length is to be used. Absolute sharpness will thus be
guaranteed, even though the long focal length may not be
needed for the shot. It is not unknown, when the lens has
been focused at its widest angle, for the image to go badly out
of focus when the zoom lever is operated.

Finally, an example of the effective difference between
the zoom and the tracking shot is seen in the closing shot of
Claude Chabrol's *La Femme Infidèle*, where a zoom-in is
matched exactly with a track-out. The area of the image
remains virtually constant throughout the shot, but the
track and the zoom working against each other have an
uncanny effect on the perspective of the shot, which shifts
in a most unsettling way. The zoom lens is used to change the
perspective, but the track-back at the same time ensures that
the image area stays the same: thus the perspective is the only
thing that changes.

Other lens effects

Focus-pulling and stop-pulling are techniques which are
often used to overcome difficulties in camerawork, rather
than to create a noticeable effect. Stop-pulling – the changing
of the aperture during a shot – becomes necessary when,
owing to camera or subject movement, the lighting conditions over the important part of the subject are significantly
changed. If, for example, a colour film with low exposure
latitude is being used for exteriors on a sunny day, and the
subject passes from bright sunlight to deep shadow, the
exposure would suffer noticeably in one of the two lighting
conditions. To compensate for this difference, it is possible

Deep focus. (*Citizen Kane*, director Orson Welles, 1948.)

to alter the exposure so as to accommodate such unavoidable differences in lighting. Stop-pulling is a two-man job: first, the exposures are calculated in the different areas, and noted by the stop-puller. The aperture is then set for the exposure required at the start of the shot, and the take begins. At the appropriate moment the camera operator will call the stop-puller, who will change the aperture to allow for the new exposure. This should be done promptly, but not too suddenly: the aim is that the effect should pass unnoticed on the screen.

Similarly, focus-pulling is frequently used to compensate for a situation in which a particular lens is unable to keep all areas of a subject in sharp focus simultaneously, or when a subject is constantly shifting and otherwise liable to go out of focus. This can be done by two operators, if all focusing distances can be worked out before the take, and the lens has an accurate focusing scale; however, with a small reflex camera, this is a job which may be more easily handled by the camera operator. A small handle clamped on to the focusing ring of the lens will make the job easier, and will also keep stray fingers from the front of the lens: the operator must bear in mind, however – since he must keep his eyes to the viewfinder – which way he must move the ring for further focus, and which way for nearer.

Focus-pulling, however, is not only used for keeping the subject in normal focus. Manipulation of the focus can be used as a creative element of the camerawork. Using limited depth of field, and changing the point of sharp focus from one area of the screen to another, can provide a very telling effect. It may be used, for example, to act as an introductory phase to a shot, or to demonstrate a series of separate elements within a shot in succession. But this again is a powerful effect which can easily be overdone.

The hand-held camera

In normal circumstances, a tripod or other rigid mount should always be used when shooting movie film. Failure to use a camera support will show up in an extreme unsteadiness of image on the screen, and will very likely be so distracting as to be unwatchable. However, there are conditions where the use of a fixed mount is impossible, for reasons of restricted space, extreme low level, or need for mobility or for speed in shooting. There are also occasions when the special effect of a hand-held camera is required for the film: perhaps to accentuate a feeling of terror or excitement, or to stand as a subjective shot after, for example, a CU of a man walking.

When using the camera hand-held, try to have available some kind of mobile support, such as a monopod – a single adjustable leg which fixes to the bottom of the camera – a 'shoulder pod', or a body-harness: these are camera mounts that are supported by the body of the camera operator. If none of these alternatives is available, there may be some convenient solid object that the camera can be rested upon – a chair, a wall or something similar. Failing all these, the camera will have to be held with the hands alone.

Hand-holding requires practice to achieve a steadiness acceptable on the screen; shaking not noticed through the viewfinder will be greatly magnified and apparent on the screen. This is particularly evident in shots that contain no movement to distract the audience's eye from the camera wobble: strong action in hand-held shots is a great advantage. If holding the camera with the hands alone, balance the body securely, grasp the camera firmly with both hands, leaving one finger free to operate the release button, and press the camera hard against the face, or any other part of the body which it touches. Different cameras, obviously, need different techniques: with the Bolex, for instance, the whole weight is borne by the operator's hands, and the camera is steadied against the face; with Arriflex and Eclair cameras the weight is chiefly borne on the shoulders, and balanced with the raised right arm. With smaller cameras like the Bolex, Beaulieu, Bell-Howell and Kodak, 'pistol-grip' type hand supports are available, and may be found to give steadier support in hand-holding. For moving with a hand-held camera, a particular gait has to be developed in order to progress with the legs while keeping the top part of the body still and smooth. The normal up-and-down movement of the body while walking should be eliminated as far as possible.

With hand-held cameras, always use as wide-angle a lens as is compatible with the required style of camerawork. The wider the angle, the less apparent will be a camera shake: the longer the focal length, the more apparent the wobble. Lenses over 50-mm. focal length, on 16-mm. cameras, are very difficult to use, and extreme telephotos of 100-mm. or over almost impossible; the reduced depth of field of long-focus lenses also adds to the problems, by making it more

Body support for hand-held
Arriflex BL.

difficult to keep a moving subject in focus. Generally, the wider the angle of the lens, the better the hand-held shooting, though, as with all shooting with very wide-angle lenses, distorting effects of camera movement should be remembered. Perhaps the best lenses to use are the 10-mm. or 16-mm. wide-angles.

Although hand-holding, being a one-man operation, makes some refinements like stop-pulling and focus-pulling difficult, it has advantages of its own – and not only practical ones like mobility and rapid shooting. Hand-holding offers a range of angles and viewpoints difficult to equal in filming from a fixed tripod, and also makes possible a great degree of intimacy between the camera and the subject. It allows a variety of material to be shot easily, and the very rapidity of the shooting keeps the cameraman's interest and excitement going, and almost always results in footage of great life and verve. But hand-held shooting of this nature also demands of the cameraman spot decisions, instantaneous choice of angle and exposure; and footage of this nature must also be expected to contain a fair proportion of less than perfect shots. And, finally, it can usually be successful only in fairly small doses, set in well-photographed surroundings, in films where it constitutes part of a pattern.

COMPOSITION AND FRAMING

The composition and framing of each shot is something that can be decided only by the cameraman's taste and judgment at the time he is lining up the shot. There is an infinite number of rules that can be drawn up about composition, but finally it will be the instinct and the experience of the cameraman which will be the decisive factor in how the take is actually shot. It is quite possible to obey all the so-called 'rules' of composition, and still come up with a shot that does not look right, or that does not fit into the plan of the film. Feeling for framing and composition is developed and felt, rather than learned from rules. Nevertheless, some of the more important considerations to bear in mind when thinking about framing will now be discussed.

First, and perhaps most important of all, is that when looking at a shot through the viewfinder, the cameraman must learn to interpret the action he sees in terms of the two-dimensional representation on the screen. What he is shooting is not two people running about in a meadow, but a red shape and a blue shape moving about on a flat background of green. Once the narrative content of the shot is decided by the director, it is no longer important to the cameraman. As noted above, the cameraman's job is not primarily a narrative one. For framing purposes, he should forget the third dimension, and work only with the first and second, and the fourth – time.

Two things are particularly helpful to the cameraman at this stage: the panchromatic viewing glass, or pan filter, and

Composition in depth and contrasting volumes. (*Ivan the Terrible*, Part I, director S. M. Eisenstein, 1936.)

the ground glass of the reflex viewfinder. The pan filter is a small piece of darkened glass that is held to the eye when looking at a scene, and which reduces the natural colour of the world to a tonal pattern, making it far easier for the cameraman to analyse the highlight-and-shadow structure of the scene before him, and to study the broad outline of his composition. The ground glass of the viewfinder (where applicable – some non-reflex cameras do not have this facility) gives very much the effect of the image projected on to a screen: the image, as seen through the lens with all the characteristic effects of that lens, is displayed on a textured surface. A director will often use a viewing glass while setting up a scene, in order to assess as well as possible the screen effect of the situation.

When framing a shot, there are an almost infinite number of details that the cameraman will notice, and which, one way or another, will influence the final decision: factors, indeed, that the audience will never even be aware of may be of prime importance to the positioning of the camera. The cameraman will note these things almost by reflex.

Ensure that all verticals appear vertical, and all horizontals appear horizontal, except when special effects are required. Tilting horizons or lop-sided houses are all too common features of careless framing. The picture, generally speaking, should not be divided by strong verticals or horizontals to the extent that it falls apart into two separate areas: it is easy for this kind of thing to happen when the cameraman is watching the action through the viewfinder, and not the visual pattern that is being created by the action. Similarly, lack of attention to the over-all image can lead to all kinds of shortcomings in the composition in the background. The classic illustration of this, of course, is the flower growing from the head of the leading lady; there, the cameraman, concentrating on filming the action, has forgotten the image and allowed the lady to stand right in front of a tall plant. The camera records this situation too faithfully, and the audience responds to the camera's record. The response is to see that the plant is springing from her head – especially if the use of a long-focus lens has condensed perspective somewhat. Backgrounds of all kinds can too easily be overlooked: yet on many occasions the background is as important in the cinematic image as is the main subject. Awareness and care are always needed.

Ensure that all visual information essential to the shot is contained within the frame, unless a specific camera movement is to be made. In this case, ensure that all relevant information is included at all stages of the movement. Adjustments of the framing during a shot in order to include a bit more information, or to improve the look of things, indicates a wrong choice of original framing, and only looks shoddy.

By and large, important actions should be kept fairly well away from the edges of the screen, although, with careful camerawork, attention can sometimes be very effectively

Superimposition. (*Strike*, director S. M. Eisenstein, 1924.)

directed to a small area near an edge or corner of a frame. The
effectiveness of this device depends in some measure on the
fact that normal technique uses the central areas of the frame
for most of the time. The edges of the frame, moreover,
should always be regarded as positive elements in the composition of the shot, not as nothing more than the point at
which the image leaves off. If the actual standard ratio frame
is unsuitable for a composition, it may well be possible to
use an element of the action to provide a natural mask within
the frame to create an altered aspect ratio, and improve the
composition.

Fill the frame: every part of the frame should play an
active part towards the whole effect, background as much as
foreground. Easy ways to waste part of the frame are to frame
too high when filming a figure (the space above the head will
probably be of little interest), or to place the main centre of
interest to one side of the frame, without using the rest of the
frame for any balancing or complementary purposes.
Always try to find the angle on the subject that allows the
most interesting use of the frame area (assuming that other
requirements, such as action necessity, or continuity, do not
prevent such an angle; in this case there will always be another
one nearly as good, or sometimes even better).

And remember that the movie camera has the enormous
advantage of being able to present its subjects convincingly
and practicably, from viewpoints that a normal pair of eyes
would seldom or never experience. This advantage should
be used: the square-on shot, from eye-level, of straight-line
action is one of the dullest ways of translating action into
screen image. Try to improve on it.

Diagonals on screen are usually strong. Movement of the
subject into the frame, especially where the scale is disguised
until the subject appears – for example, an apparent long-
shot of a landscape into which a face moves in big close up –
is dynamic. Visual mystery, unravelled during the progress
of the shot, can be a strong device, though tension should not
be allowed to drop by delaying the explanation for too long:
timing is important. The effect on the audience is: first,
registering of the impact of a strong visual image; second, a
moment of puzzlement as to what it might be (after a very
short time, the identity of the image should be revealed,
perhaps by a slight zoom-out, or a short camera movement);
and, finally, realization of identity and relation of the part to
the whole. Visual surprise, either where there is a sudden
movement into the frame, especially from the bottom, or
else where the visual image turns out to be different from the
audience's initial assumption, is a similar stimulant to the
camerawork of the film. Short camera movements, from an
'introductory' image to the main subject of the shot, or a
pull focus of the same nature; marked distortion caused by
deliberate use of extreme lenses; strong foreground interest,
not only in long-shot but in close-up too; filming through
very close out-of-focus foreground; use of reflections, and

relating them to their source: these, and many more, are ideas that a cameraman will sort through with his director, and possibly with his script-writer, when deciding on the framing of the individual shot.

With any composition, however careless, there will be one or more focal points of the audience's attention; these must be assessed by the cameraman, and their exact position arranged both for the best visual effect, and for smooth co-ordination with surrounding shots. The focus of attention is affected in four ways.

Highlight and shadow distribution. The eye is strongly drawn to the main highlight as soon as the picture appears on the screen (though when the screen is predominantly white, it may be the intense shadow that attracts). Since the attraction is strong, the distribution of highlights on the screen, and their relation to the position of the main action, are of great importance. Normally, the highlight would be used to reinforce the main action, but visual mystery and tension could perhaps be increased by keeping important action away from the areas to which the eye is naturally drawn. Think forward to the editing of the film when considering the distribution of highlights in the frame: if the editor is to cut the scene smoothly, he will want to be able to match highlights in one shot with highlights in the next, so that the audience's eyes are not continually dragged round the screen.

Movement. Generally, the stronger the movement, the more it will attract attention. However, in many compositions, there will be subsidiary patterns of movement, e.g. a crowd in the background, or traffic passing by. These subsidiary actions must be clearly noted, for where other things are equal, it may be one of these subsidiary movements that is used by the editor to draw the audience's eyes to the required screen position for the cut to the next shot.

Colour. Reds attract most strongly; yellows also attract more quickly than greens and blues.

The *visual bias* of the composition can lead the eye forcefully to any required area of the frame.

All of these factors can be used together, or in opposition, but they must be recognized, and an analysis of their presence in the proposed shot is one of the main tasks of camerawork.

Filters

The use of filters has a vital effect on the appearance of the photographic image, and the choice of filter is one of the responsibilities of the cameraman in finalizing the composition of the shot. There are two basic types of filter – the colour-correction (CC) filter and the B/W filter. Colour correction filters are used with colour film to produce the best colour renderings under given light conditions, by slightly altering the colour of the light reaching the film. The most commonly used CC filters are those designed to balance daylight film for exposure to tungsten light, and for exposing artificial-light film to daylight. Used without a filter, an artificial-light film exposed in daylight will give colours that appear excessively blue. By using a filter that cuts out some of the blue light reaching the film, the balance of the film is restored, and the colour rendering is made more natural. Colour-correction filters can also, of course, be used to distort colours for special purposes: for example, a light green or yellow filter might be used to exaggerate the green-ness of a lyrical woodland or meadow scene.

Black-and-white filters generally affect the tone repro-duction of a b/w film, where different colour filters will emphasize different tones. A yellow filter, for example, with a b/w film, will give a much better rendering of the sky in exteriors, for by keeping out much of the intense blue light from the sky, it prevents the overexposure normal on the sky part of the image, and gives good detail in cloud forma-tions etc. A red filter may exaggerate the sky detail to a con-siderable extent and may be useful for a particular mood. A green filter will emphasize green areas, while reducing the effect of red areas; and so on, through a wide range of filters.

There is a further range of filters which do not so much alter the effect of the light on the film, as make filming in certain conditions more reliable and successful. The ultra-violet (UV) filter, which is almost completely clear, has no effect on the tone or colour of the image, but cuts out ultra-violet light, which can often create a haze in, for example, exterior long-shots. Polarizing filters, or Pola-screens, cut the glare from reflected light, and reduce the flare in *contre-jour* filming. Neutral density (ND) filters are neutral in light-transmission characteristics, but cut down the amount of light transmitted to a determined extent. These filters have wide application, both where light is too bright to obtain a satisfactory exposure (for example, when using a very fast film on sunlit exteriors), or when the cameraman desires to use a wider aperture than his normal exposure calculations would allow (for instance to decrease the depth of field of a lens in order to achieve a differential focus effect). Neutral density filters are available in many densities, from the equi-valent of one stop less exposure, to heavy filters cutting light transmission several times.

All filters are made to exact specifications of light trans-mission, so that the cameraman can know for certain the amount of light that any given filter will prevent from reach-ing the film, and adjust his exposure accordingly. Each filter has a filter factor, expressed in terms of the number of times the exposure must be multiplied to produce the equivalent exposure (see p. 59). The factor of any filter, or combination of filters – an ND filter and a yellow filter, for example, may well be used simultaneously – must be taken into considera-tion when calculating exposure. Filters should be studied carefully, for the improvement brought by careful use of appropriate filters can vastly improve the quality of the camerawork.

9 Continuity

Continuity is, strictly speaking, a responsibility shared by script-writer, director, cameraman and editor. However, the decisions made during the actual shooting of the film are those that are really crucial to continuity, and these are largely made by the cameraman, with, of course, the director's over-all control. It is the cameraman above all who must be aware of the needs of continuity, especially in small-unit filming, where there will probably be no full-time continuity girl to remind the director and cameraman of details that might slip their notice. In case of uncertainty, however, the best person to ask for advice is the editor. He will know, from bitter experience, just how much difference can be made by a small positional adjustment in shooting, for instance; and the right advice at the right time can save a retake, or a rather obvious use of 'cutaway' in editing (see below, p. 83).

Continuity can be divided into four main areas: continuity of action, continuity of place, continuity of time, and photographic continuity. But these are not areas that can be looked at separately when actually constructing a shot: one interacts with another, and all may play a part in the shooting of a sequence. Points about time continuity lead directly to points of action continuity, and so on. Thus, although continuity can be divided for convenience of reference, an over-all concept must emerge.

CONTINUITY OF TIME

An impression of continuous and convincing 'time' must always be built up in a film. Screen time is very rarely the same thing as real time, and so a means must be found of bridging the gaps that must be left in real time in its translation to the screen, and of maintaining a convincing flow in the progression of the film. The problem is normally caused by the need to shorten real time; but it can work the other way. A legitimate device in the cinema is to prolong a moment to heighten its impact and significance – the moment of the opening of the bridge in the 'Raising of the Bridges' sequence in Eisenstein's *October* is one well-known example. In this sequence, one of the images is of a dead woman's hair slipping from one half of the bridge to the other as the halves part and raise: the initial slipping action is in fact repeated several times, intercut with other images. Real time of, say, two seconds is extended in the sequence to something nearer two minutes.

But, more frequently, it is the need to condense time for the screen that poses continuity problems. There are a number of standard devices for achieving this, although it should be added that there is a developing acceptance of ellipsis in screen time, and less elaborate measures for shortening time are increasingly used. As with all film problems, the final test is, does it look right on the screen? If it does, theory can often be dispensed with. Firstly, fades and dissolves can easily do away with long sections of time – 'long' in this sense, of course, relatively to the nature of the subject-matter of the film. A mere few minutes may be a large break in one film, whereas a fade-out and fade-in can easily cover a number of years (or even centuries, as in Kubrick's *2001*). The audience will always accept the film-maker's word for how much time has elapsed during a fade or a dissolve: the one thing that the film-maker must do, is to let the audience know how much time has gone, if it is of any importance. Certain effects of sound editing can also be used to cover broad areas of time. The employment of fades, dissolves etc. in this way is part of the editor's job.

It is the condensation of apparent on-screen time from real time to screen time that calls for particular care by the cameraman. Most actions will be too long to show in their entirety, and would not hold the audience's interest anyway. Time can be reduced merely by showing the beginning and end of the action, but, although this may seem the simplest course of action, it is often very difficult to do successfully. Such a cut from beginning to end, omitting the middle, must be accompanied by a radical change of angle and composition, in order to distract the attention for a while from the action that is not continuous, possibly reinforcing the change of angle by a move from CU to LS or vice versa. If this manœuvre is not done well, the result will almost inevitably be a jump-cut, which will disrupt the flow of the sequence.

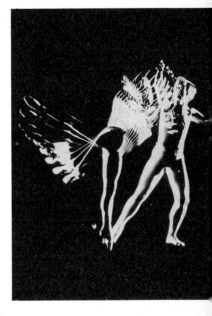

Multiple image; note also the extreme low-key rim lighting. (*Pas de Deux*, director Norman Maclaren, 1968.)

The usual way of overcoming the problem of condensing action is to use a 'cutaway' shot – a shot of anything related to the main action but not actually including it – between the beginning of the action and the end. The cutaway shot, moreover, may also be a 'reaction' shot, showing the reaction of one or more of the film's protagonists to the action, and thus guiding the audience's response, either to the action or to the person. For example: a sequence about getting a car ready for the big race, with the mechanics battling against time. The whole operation of screwing on the carburettors would obviously take five or ten minutes, and certainly could not be shown complete. So a shot is taken of the mechanic starting the operation, followed by a cutaway of a clock, followed by a CU of his face, concentrating and anxious, and then a final shot of him tightening the last screw and straightening up. This sequence will appear as a natural and convincing portrayal of the real time. Thirty seconds will have been made to stand for ten minutes or more. What the film is in fact doing is setting up a representation of time, much as it sets up a representation of places and people. Although this kind of continuity is largely the editor's responsibility, the cameraman must be well aware of it if he is to bring home the right shots, especially when he is filming without a script.

CONTINUITY OF PLACE

It is important that the audience should always feel sure about the locations of the action, and that no apparent discrepancies in the visual presentation occur to unsettle the audience's conviction of those locations. A typical lapse that can occur in this field is when differing light conditions from different shooting sessions are intercut into a scene that is intended to appear continuous. Shadows at different angles, for instance, or shadows that appear and disappear from shot to shot, are the kind of thing that is easily overlooked. Equally important are details of settings, which must be absolutely consistent from session to session if the results are to be intercut: this problem is particularly severe in the case of retakes. If, in an exterior scene, for example, a parked car is visible in the background, it must remain there for all subsequent shots, unless it is seen to drive off; its sudden disappearance (and, worse still, re-appearance) will be most noticeable on the screen. A continuity girl – a position which demands a high level of foresight and concentration – must keep records of all such details; if things have unavoidably altered by the time of the second session, the cameraman will have to take care to keep all signs of the alterations off the screen. The same consideration applies equally, of course, to every detail of dress, make-up, personal appearance, as well as to every minor prop.

Further, if a particular aspect of a location is to be shown, it must be established as part of the general scene. This can be done either by showing a general 'establishing' shot of the whole location, so that the audience can place all component parts, or else by tying in the detail with a correct 'eyeline'. If neither of these links is made, it may seem on screen as if the action has moved to another location.

The tying in of detail by the use of eyeline and suggestion has a particular advantage: it can be quite easily used to make it appear that a particular object is actually at the location in use, when in fact it was filmed at an entirely different time and place. There are many applications of this effect: one good example is the common scene where the intrepid hero (or the young boy) is confronted by a wild snarling panther (or a lion or puma or tiger or snake). All shots of the panther are taken from the angle at which the audience supposes the hero would see it; and all shots of the hero are taken with him looking either towards the camera, with the camera at the height of the panther's eyes, or else off-screen to where the audience assumes the panther to be. When these shots are intercut, they will convincingly show the hero and the panther in the same place at the same time.

The same effect is equally convincing in less dramatic situations. If a person in MCU suddenly turns his head and looks off-screen, the next shot, provided it is taken at the angle from which the audience expects the person on screen to have been looking, will automatically be assumed to be what that person was looking at, unless there is strong evidence to negate the impression. Similarly with doors: if a man goes through a door, the next shot will tend to be taken for the place into which he has gone. If the same man is shown in another room – even if it is in fact on a completely different location – the assumption will usually be that he has walked straight from one room into the next. This whole process has almost infinite possibilities, which are continually explored during film-making. Skilful camerawork and editing can produce or adapt the most unlikely locations.

PHOTOGRAPHIC CONTINUITY

This aspect of continuity has already been briefly touched on in the discussion of exposure (see p. 59). Because of the immediate and uninterrupted succession of images in movie film, consistency of visual texture is essential if the sequence is to flow smoothly and be accepted as being of one piece. There are, however, other factors to watch for, in addition to consistency of exposure. First, the filmstock should be the same throughout (except where deliberate visual effect is sought), otherwise variations in grain structure or contrast, which can be marked between one stock and another, will show up. Particular care must be taken with colour stocks, as colour renderings differ radically; in fact it is probably safe to say that different colour filmstocks should *never* be intercut. Even some stocks with apparently similar names can give very different interpretations of colour (see p. 41), and the changes on the screen can be most alarming.

Second, lighting must be consistent from one shot to the next. The lighting of each shot is a vital part of its visual identity; even a small spotlight apparently disappearing between shots will alter the visual nature of the shot, and create disruption in continuity. Therefore, when shooting a scene in the studio in more than one session, it is a good idea to draw up a diagram of the major lighting set-ups so that all details are consistent from one session to the next. The references may also be useful for the setting up of retakes.

In all its forms, photographic continuity is the responsibility of the cameraman.

CONTINUITY OF ACTION

This is probably the most involved aspect of continuity, and the area where, as the elements are not always so evident, slips are most easily made. Continuity of action is basically the construction and fitting together of several successive shots in such a manner that the audience assumes that the action portrayed in them is continuous, and so that it flows naturally and without pause from one shot to another. This involves, principally, continuity of direction of movement, and the preservation of eyelines. The traditional methods of achieving these ends are described at some length in Joseph V. Mascelli's *The Five C's of Cinematography*. The art of placing the camera so that movement appears consistent from shot to shot, and eyelines tie up correctly, is illustrated with many examples, and, for the traditional answers to the problems, this can be a useful book.

In all cases the visual expectancy aroused in an audience by a shot must be understood, and must be satisfied in the following shot. If a man is walking from left to right on the screen in the first shot in which he appears, he must continue to move in this direction in all subsequent shots, unless he is seen to change direction, or unless a change in direction is strongly implied. Walking directly towards, or away from, the camera is normally neutral, and can be used in conjunction with either direction. This premise is extended to cover all forms of directional movement on the screen. When movement is square on to the camera, it is fairly easy to keep directional continuity; but where the movement is diagonal (as it frequently is, especially when the subject passes close by the camera), confusion can arise as to where to place the camera for the next shot. The guideline for maintaining successful continuity is to draw an imaginary line along the axis of the action, and always keep the camera to the same side of this line. Crossing this axis ('crossing the eyeline') will result in apparent reversal of direction of movement.

The principle of 'eyeline' is also tied up with continuity of direction. 'Eyeline' again denotes the fulfilment of visual expectancy, in that any shot must be presented from the angle of view suggested by the previous shot. The most obvious example of this is in the intercutting of cu's of two people talking to each other; if one person is looking off-screen towards his interlocutor, this second person's look must tie in with that of the first person. Thus, if a man is talking to a woman, he may be looking off-screen downwards and to the right: the shot of the woman must show her looking upwards and to the left. Again in this case the camera must never cross the axis of the action, or both people will appear to be speaking in the same direction, and not to each other: their apparent spatial relationship on the screen will not reflect their real one.

The principle of 'eyeline' also applies to inanimate objects that have a spatial relationship with each other, and to the interrelationship between an animate and an inanimate object. For example, if a man looks up at a sign, that sign must be shot from a low angle, the angle that the man would see it from – not straight on or from a high angle. Eyeline is also closely related to continuity of place in some instances, especially in the location of inanimate objects.

Directional continuity and eyelines must be carefully preserved in all shooting, and call for care and constant attention from the cameraman. Lapses in continuity of this kind will cause a temporary lack of orientation in the audience, and this will invariably be damaging to the total effect. An editor may be able to patch up occasional errors in continuity of action with tactful use of cutaways or specially shot retakes; in some circumstances he can even use wrong eyelines to create deliberate tension. However, sound basic camerawork must always include the ability to create cohesion in this aspect, as in all others, of continuity.

TITLES

Graphics is a large subject in its own right, and is covered in another book in the present series.* A single paragraph must be included here, however, to emphasize the extreme importance of titles to a film, and the need to prepare and film all the graphic content of the film with meticulous care and attention. The titles must be thought of as one of the vital sequences of the film – not as an afterthought to be quickly filmed and stuck on when all other work is finished. Even if the titles are merely unambitious Letraset or type-set wording, great pains should be taken to see that all the lettering is done well, and filmed absolutely squarely on the screen. Use fine-grain, high-contrast filmstock: it may even be worth having the titles shot by the labs, if adequate titling camera facilities are not available. This is often as cheap as doing them in the film unit, especially for short lengths of titles which would necessitate short-ending a roll of film. Titles do much to set the tone of the film: that they should be done well is of the highest priority.

* *The Thames & Hudson Manual of Television Graphics* by Ron Hurrell.

10 Sound recording

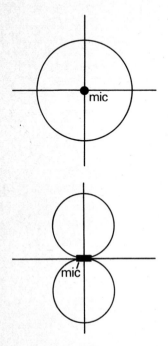

Polar diagrams for omnidirectional (*top*) and figure-of-eight microphones.

The sound-track is almost as important to the finished film as the picture. A sound-track is not something that can be added to a finished picture print just to give it a boost: it is scripted carefully from the early stages of the film. To do the sound-track justice, the film-maker must ensure that all sound recording, transfer and dubbing are of the highest quality. The picture of the finished print will be printed direct from the master film, and there will be little room for significant loss of quality; with the sound-track, however, the recording that appears on the married release print will have been transferred from one recording medium to another at least three times – from $\frac{1}{4}$-in. tape to 16-mm. film, from separate magnetic tracks to mixed master, and from mixed magnetic master to magnetic edge stripe on the married print or optical negative track – and then printed; and at each stage there could well have been loss of quality. It is evident, therefore, that the original sound recording must be of the highest possible quality, if the sound on the final print is to be satisfactory.

Sound recording, however, is probably the most technically complex operation involved in the making of a film, requiring a basic knowledge of acoustics and electronics for complete understanding. Fortunately, for everyday operation of sound recorders it is not essential to understand all the electronic details of the process, as long as the correct procedures are known. It is possible to record successfully without knowing an ohm from an elephant, so long as it is known that impedances on all pieces of equipment must be matched, and that impedances are marked in ohms. Extreme care and trouble should, however, be taken with the recording of sound. As with every department of film-making, the achievement of high quality should be one of the aims, and one of the pleasures, of the film-maker, and he should study how to get the best possible results from his equipment.

There are three stages, and three items of equipment in the tape-recording layout: the pickup of the signal and its conversion into electrical currents (the microphone); the amplification of the signal to a degree at which its effect can be conveniently recorded (the amplifier); and the recording itself (the recording-head).

Each part of this chain is essential, and the quality of the recording can only be as good as the quality of the worst piece of equipment. If a poor microphone is used, for example, the recording will be correspondingly poor, no matter how excellent the amplifier and recorder.

The *microphone* is a device for converting sound waves into electrical impulses. Microphones are divided into two basic categories, according to their directional response (i.e. the range of directions from which they pick up sound), which is inherent in their design. The two types are: *omnidirectional*, which are sensitive to sound waves coming from all directions, and which can be represented by a polar diagram, and *figure-of-eight* microphones, which are sensitive to sound waves only in front of or behind them.

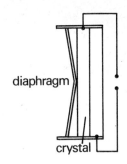

OMNIDIRECTIONAL	FIGURE-OF-EIGHT
crystal	ribbon
condenser	
moving-coil (dynamic)	

Crystal microphones. Certain crystals, when compressed or distorted, emit electrical impulses in proportion to the amount of distortion. In a crystal microphone, the diaphragm is deflected by the pressure of the sound waves, and in turn compresses the crystal, either by direct contact or by air pressure. Since this microphone is activated by pressure, the response is omnidirectional

The crystal microphone is always high impedance, and is rarely used for work of a professional standard: it is mainly confined to the amateur market.

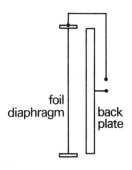

The condenser microphone is fed a direct-current voltage; the sound waves cause the foil diaphragm to fluctuate, and the capacity of the condenser formed by the foil diaphragm and the back-plate changes according to these fluctuations. The changes in the condenser produce changes in the applied voltage which is fed to the amplifier. Again, since this microphone operates on pressure, its response is omnidirectional.

In *moving-coil* or *dynamic microphones* the movement of the diaphragm causes a coil to move along the magnetic field of a permanent magnet; this induces a varying current in the coil, in proportion to the pressure of the soundwaves. Again, this microphone is omnidirectional.

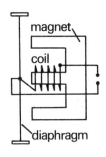

Ribbon microphones constitute the majority of figure-of-eight mikes. A foil ribbon is suspended in the magnetic field of a permanent magnet, and vibrates in accordance with the sound waves that fall upon it. This movement within the magnetic field induces a varying current in the ribbon, which is in turn fed to the amplifier. Since this microphone works on pressure gradient, i.e. the difference in pressure in front of and behind the ribbon, the response is along one axis only, and falls in a figure of eight on the polar diagram.

The ribbon microphone is very sensitive indeed, and can sometimes be over-sensitive to sharp sounds; it may not, for instance, be suitable for recording speech from a close range.

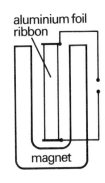

The four main types of microphone. Reading downwards: crystal microphone, condenser microphone, moving-coil or 'dynamic' microphone, ribbon microphone.

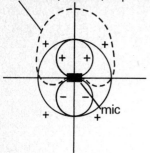

combined (cardioid) response

mic

Polar diagram of the cardioid microphone.

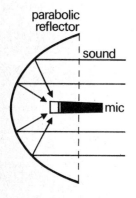

parabolic reflector

sound

mic

Parabolic reflector with omni-directional microphone.

Sennheifer 805 rifle microphone with windshield.

A further type of response can be obtained by a combination of an omnidirectional and a figure-of-eight microphone. This produces a unidirectional microphone, which derives its usual name, cardioid, from its heart-shaped polar diagram. This works because the response behind a figure-of-eight microphone is 180° out-of-phase with the response in front. When this is combined with an omnidirectional response, which is in the same phase all round, the responses behind the microphone cancel out, and those in front add, giving the characteristic heart-shaped response.

It is also possible to make combined microphones: these have three-way switches giving the option of omnidirectional, figure-of-eight or cardioid responses. Even more directional responses than those obtained with normal cardioid microphones can be arranged, for example with either 'rifle' mikes – often cardioid microphones fitted with a tube to reduce the area of response to the minimum – or with microphones situated at the focus of a parabolic reflector which reflects sound waves back on to the microphone itself.

Impedance. Microphones will be either of a high or a low impedance, and it is essential to know which. Impedance is a fairly involved subject, but can be loosely described as the resistance presented to an alternating current (in fact it is a combination of DC resistance, inductance and capacitance). As the impedance affects the amount of current carried at any given voltage, it is very important to match the impedance of the microphone to that of the recorder input. The classic analogy with the water-pipe will make this clear.

In the diagram opposite, the water represents the electric current, the width of the pipe the impedance, and the eddies in the water flow represent distortion. The current flowing through the wide pipe (low impedance, letting a large amount of current through) comes to a point where the size of the pipe is reduced considerably (high impedance, capable of bearing only a part of the current at the same rate of flow). The only possible result is that some of the current must eddy back, and this causes distortion in the current,

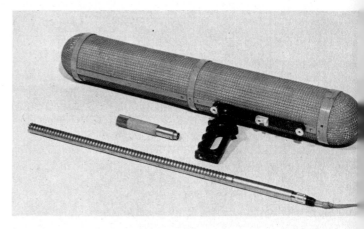

and thus, in a recording set-up, distortion of some kind in the signal fed from microphone to recording-head.

Most professionally used microphones are of a low impedance, and these have the advantage that they can be used with a long length of cable between microphone and input without signal fall-off (some portable recorders, particularly, do use high-impedance microphones); it is essential that low-impedance microphones be fed into low-impedance inputs. If a low-impedance microphone is to be used with a high-impedance input, a matching transformer must be used to adapt the current flow. In some set-ups, such as a Reslo 50/60 ohm low-impedance microphone used with a Ferrograph recorder, an adaptor is available to fit directly on to the microphone cable; otherwise the cable must be plugged into the transformer, and the transformer to the recorder input. Failure to match impedances of equipment will result in loss or distortion of signal.

The *amplifier* in a recording system is simply a standard amplifier to amplify the weak signal received from the microphone to a degree sufficient to activate the recording process. This stage of the recorder's work can be taken for granted.

After the signal has been amplified, it is fed to the *recording-heads*. These are simply small electromagnets, with a very fine gap between the poles. The signal from the amplifier is fed to the coil in the head, and the fluctuations in the signal current cause changes in the magnetic field around the gap. These changes are recorded on the magnetic tape passing across the head. The tape consists of a fine, flexible plastic base coated with ferrous oxide; the oxide is magnetized to varying degrees as it passes across the recording head, according to the state of the magnetic field around the tape in the head.

Replaying is the reverse of the recording operation. The tape, already magnetized, is drawn across the head, and the changes in the magnetic field on the tape induce varying currents in the coil of the replay head. The currents thus induced are amplified, and fed out to the loudspeaker, which is the reverse of the microphone, and which converts the electrical impulses, via a vibrating diaphragm, to sound waves.

There are two other mechanical factors that affect the quality of the sound recording, quite apart from the quality of the amplifier.

Magnetic recording tape is manufactured on a number of different bases – acetate, polyester, PVC etc. The different thicknesses of these materials enable manufacturers to create what are known as 'standard', 'long-play' and 'extra-play' (or comparable terms, varying from manufacturer to manufacturer), indicating the length of time that can be recorded on the standard reel sizes. Long-play and extra-play tapes are chiefly used by the amateur market: the thinner tape bases, although stable enough for their intended

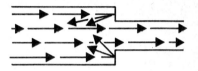

Impedance: the analogy with a water-pipe.

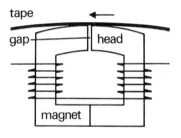

Record/replay-head.

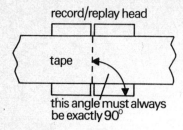

record/replay head

tape

this angle must always
be exactly 90°

Azimuth: the angle between the gap
of the head and the direction of
travel of the tape.

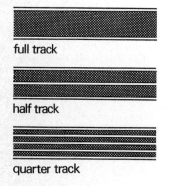

full track

half track

quarter track

Track configurations for ¼-in. tape.

purposes, are not suitable for high-quality sound recording at high running speeds, and are more liable to stretch. Only standard-play tapes should be used for sound recording for films.

Within the standard ¼-in. width of the magnetic recording tape, there are three configurations of recorded areas, or track arrangements, resulting from the arrangement of the heads on the tape recorder – full-track, half-track, quarter-track. Professional-quality recorders normally use either full-track recording, for maximum signal-to-noise ratio (i.e. the highest proportion of wanted recording signal to the background noise inherent in the tape and the recording system) and quality in recording; or half-track, which still gives a good signal-to-noise ratio, but is more economical with tape, since each reel is used twice along its length, once in each direction of travel. Some sync pulse systems (see below) also use half-track recording. Quarter-track recording is seldom used for film work.

The running speed of the tape directly affects the frequency response of the recording: the faster the tape travels, the higher the frequencies that can be recorded. Standard running speeds are: $1\frac{7}{8}$ inches per second, $3\frac{3}{4}$ i.p.s., $7\frac{1}{2}$ i.p.s., 15 i.p.s. and 30 i.p.s. For the very highest quality of recording, say studio music recording, 30 or 15 i.p.s. may be used, but for most film work $7\frac{1}{2}$ i.p.s. is used. This is fast enough to give excellent response and frequency range, but also gives a reasonable economy in use, and is easier to handle when editing. The use of very high-speed tape on small portable machines such as are frequently used for film location work would also mean that tapes would need to be changed very frequently, at considerable inconvenience.

Finally, the tape must be driven at a precisely constant speed: this is a function of the recorder motor. If there is any fluctuation at all in tape speed, the signal, when played back, will give a distorted account of the sound that should have been recorded, most probably in the form of 'wow' – an unsteadiness in the pitch of the sound. A further advantage of a fast tape speed is that any momentary variation in tape speed will only cover a small fraction of the sound being recorded, whereas with a slow speed, the same amount of tape will contain much more signal, and so more signal will be distorted.

In the *recording-heads* there are two factors affecting the quality of sound reproduction: first, the narrower the gap between the poles of the magnet, the higher the frequencies that can be recorded; second, the 'azimuth', the alignment between the gap of the head and the direction of travel of the tape, must be exactly the same in recording and replay units. The standard angle is 90° between the vertical line drawn through the gap of the magnet, and the horizontal of the direction of travel of the tape.

If the azimuth is not correctly adjusted, and the azimuth of the recording instrument is different from that of the play-back machine, there will be a loss of signal, in proportion to the degree of error in alignment. This factor is in fact used to adjust the azimuth: a tape with a standard azimuth is put through the machine, and the head adjusted until maximum output is achieved.

SYNCHRONOUS SOUND RECORDING

All the above descriptions and remarks apply equally to all kinds of sound recording for every purpose. There is a peculiar consideration, however, which arises only in connection with film work – that of keeping the sound recorded in synchronization with a moving picture being filmed. Since magnetic recording tape stretches, slips and so on, it is not sufficient merely to record the sound at the same time as the picture is shot: on replay the variations in the physical condition of the tape, together with mechanical variations, however slight, on the different pieces of equipment used, will mean that exact synchronization will be lost very quickly, and, especially with voices on screen, the sound will be unusable. Various systems are therefore used in much film sound work to keep film and magnetic $\frac{1}{4}$-in. tape together during shooting, so that the sound can be fitted exactly to the picture. This process is called synchronous sound recording or, more usually, shooting sync.

Synchronous sound recording can be subdivided into two categories: $\frac{1}{4}$-in. systems using $\frac{1}{4}$-in. tape, and systems using 16-mm. magnetic film. One way of recording sound synchronously with the picture is to use perforated $\frac{1}{4}$-in. tape on a special recorder. The drive of the tape recorder is linked to that of the camera, either mechanically by a flexible drive cable, or electrically, and the tape is driven by sprockets rather than the usual $\frac{1}{4}$-in. capstan drive system. This system is in fact now virtually defunct, and the more versatile pulse-sync system is now practically standard.

The pulse-sync system uses an almost standard $\frac{1}{4}$-in. tape recorder, and the variations in the speed of the tape caused by stretch and slip, which would normally cause the sound and picture to lose sync, are dealt with by recording on the tape, along with the sound, a pulse generated by the camera itself. The tape is replayed on a variable-speed machine, and its speed varied to keep the pulse constant. This ensures that when the sound is transferred to 16-mm. magnetic film for editing, the sound is exactly synchronous,

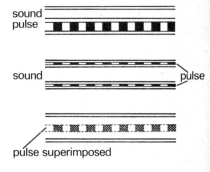

sound
pulse

sound pulse

pulse superimposed

Different sync-pulse layouts.

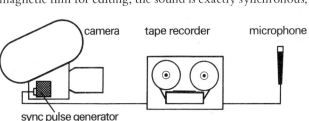

camera   tape recorder   microphone

sync pulse generator

Layout for pulse-sync recording.

Arriflex BL with commag. sound-recording module: general view and close-up.

frame for frame, with the picture. The actual recording of the pulse can be in one of several positions on the tape, according to the type of recorder used. In the last configuration, the pulse is recorded over part of the same area covered by the main signal, but at a different azimuth so that it needs a specially adjusted head to replay, and does not affect replay of the main signal. This system, used on the very popular Nagra recorders, allows full-track recording to be used for maximum sound quality.

The pulse-sync system has several advantages over all other systems. Perhaps the chief of these is convenience: the lightness of the equipment, its portable construction and battery operation make location sync shooting a relatively easy task. Long cables can be used, making it possible for camera operator and sound recordist to remain some distance apart; in some systems there is no direct link between camera and recorder – either a common pulse-generator can be used, or the crystal sync, operated by matching crystals in both camera and recorder which oscillate at precisely the same rate: in this case no link at all is required between camera and recorder.

Other advantages of pulse sync include cost – compared with 16-mm. sepmag. systems, both equipment prices and running costs are low – and quality: the separate $\frac{1}{4}$-in. magnetic tape system of recording produces the highest-quality results available.

16-mm. magnetic film systems can be subdivided into 'commag.' (combined magnetic sound) and 'sepmag.' (separate magnetic sound). In the commag. system the raw filmstock used has a magnetic stripe on the non-sprocket edge. The film passes through the camera gate and then on to a recording system which puts the sound signal direct onto the stripe. The film then returns to the take-up spool. Only the recording-heads are placed within the camera body: the microphone and amplifier are carried by the sound recordist, and the signal fed into the camera input.

The main use of this system is for news or interview work, where speed of processing is the main consideration. Master material shot in this way can be edited directly, and projected with sync sound without delay for transfer and dubbing processes. The main disadvantage of commag. recording is the poor general quality, both of signal response and of stability. Also, the sound is recorded on 16-mm. stock, 26 frames in advance of the related picture. This causes great difficulty when cutting the combined picture and film: the only solution is to re-record the sound from the stripe on the separate 16-mm. magnetic film, which entails a further quality loss.

The sepmag. system obtains synchronization by recording direct on to 16-mm. perforated magnetic film, as used in sound editing, on a special recorder, which is linked – either by the frequency of the current supply or by the Sel-syn system of interlocking motor drives – to the motor of the camera. This system is widely used in studio work, but is too bulky for general location work; moreover, the equipment is very expensive, and does not often feature in small-unit 16-mm. production.

RECORDING PROCEDURE

Assuming that the correct equipment is available, and that it is of a good standard, the quality of recording will depend on:

    the type of microphone
    the placing of the microphone
    the acoustics of the recording area
    the adjustment of the recorder
    the nature of the sound being recorded

These considerations will vary according to the broad class of sound being recorded, which is usually divided, for reference, into speech, music and effects (FX).

The most commonly used microphone for *speech* recording is the ribbon microphone, though this has a drawback in that, if it is placed too close to the mouth of the speaker the bass content of the voice is over-emphasized; specially compensated ribbon microphones are, however, available for speech recording.

Moving-coil microphones are also widely used for recording speech. These are generally satisfactory, but can emphasize sibilance (the *ss* and *sh* sounds in speech) if used too closely.

Microphones will invariably be mounted indirectly, suspended in their supports by rubber straps or other shock-absorbers. The main types of support are a stand – either a table-stand or a floor-stand, which will be telescopic, and have a heavy base – or a boom. There are many types of boom, from simple 'fish-pole' types to large and complex self-propelling ones. The main essentials of a boom are adjustability of length, angle of tilt, and rotation of microphone. A simple home-made boom might be a broom handle with the microphone tied on one end, while a typical professional studio boom will have all functions controlled by wires, pulleys and handles, and may even be motorized.

Recording speech needs care. It is important to render a clear and natural sound, but there will necessarily be some degree of colouring from the acoustics of the location, and this must be carefully assessed and integrated into the recording pattern. Ideally, for speech, the recording room should be the size of an average living-room. The floor and the walls should be equally absorbent – the floor being carpeted. In practice, an average living-room with carpets and plenty of soft furnishings is about right, but most actual recording locations, if not in specially prepared studios, are very far removed from this ideal. Bearing in mind the feel of the average living-room, the sound recordist can begin to adapt his actual location by means of either prepared acoustic aids, or by makeshift stand-ins. Sound-absorbing screens – panels of wood covered on one side by acoustic tiles – are a simple and effective means of controlling acoustics: if such devices are not available, blankets, coats or rugs hung around the speaker may make an excellent substitute.

In a large, echo-y room, experiments should be made with screens in order to obtain the best acoustics: trial of set-ups is the only sure way to get the best from any situation. An arrangement that is often successful in a large room is that of a V-formation in front of and behind the speaker, using a ribbon microphone.

In a small room there may be unwanted resonance from bare walls, giving a generally 'live' acoustic characteristic to the room. Here again screens or cloth 'fluffs' can be used to deaden the acoustics, or perhaps a directional microphone might be employed, and angled to cut out as many as possible of the unwanted sound reflections. Again experiment and adjustment, together with experience and judgment, will produce the best results. A useful guide to the acoustic characteristics of the location is to record a hand-clap. It should die away fairly quickly, without sounding muffled, and in no circumstances should it echo or ring.

The microphone should be placed on the same level as the lips, and approximately two feet away from them. If it is nearer, it will emphasize the sibilance or bass, according to type: if further away, the recording will sound echo-y and hollow, and ambient noise (i.e. other unwanted sounds) will increase in relation to the voice. If the speaker is sitting at a table, the microphone should be mounted on a table-

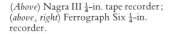

(*Above*) Nagra III ¼-in. tape recorder;
(*above, right*) Ferrograph Six ¼-in.
recorder.

stand, and the table surface should be covered with absorbent material so that there are no unwanted reflections from that direction.

Once the microphone is positioned, and the acoustics adapted to requirements, important remaining adjustments should be to the tape recorder: the selection of running speed and the setting of the record level. The record-level indicator will either be the 'magic-eye' type (mostly on cheaper instruments), in which two illuminated areas move towards the centre of a scale from either end, according to intensity of signal, or a VU meter type, which will have the maximum level of signal desirable marked on the scale. In the case of the magic-eye type, the gain (record level) adjuster should be set to the point where the two illuminated strips just touch in the centre of the indicator, at the loudest point of the sound to be recorded: with the VU meter type, the needle should peak (i.e. reach its highest position) at the recommended mark. If the signal is allowed to exceed the levels indicated on the meter, distortion in the recording will occur. If the signal is not strong enough to send the indicator to the correct peaking point, then the maximum recording quality will not be obtained.

Some recorders – e.g. the Nagra III – have an automatic signal-level setting, and will compensate for any level of sound fed into the microphone. This facility can be very useful, especially with hand-held sync shooting, or in situations where there is no time to check signal level between each take. There is, however, a slight fall-off in response if this device is used, and in some situations the automatic compensation can have unusual effects. For example, in a situation where a voice is talking over drumbeats, the automatic facility will compensate to keep the over-all signal level constant, so that for the duration of each drumbeat the level of the voice will be depressed, creating a noticeable fluctuation in the voice.

There are two ways of approaching this: recording commentary 'wild', and recording the commentary cued to the picture. Recording wild, the commentator merely reads the commentary script without attempting to relate it to any picture, though the speed of delivery may be estimated beforehand. The completed commentary is then fitted to the picture on the bench, and the pauses filled out with unmodulated (i.e. virgin) track. The main disadvantage of this method is, of course, that it cannot be judged till later how well the commentary is fitting to the picture: if certain sections are too long, they may have to be re-recorded. However, in a film where there is not very much commentary, this system has much to commend it. If no soundproof room is available for recording, there is no worry about the noise of the projector recording on the tape; presentation will not be marred by distractions such as cue-marks. And it is much more straightforward. If a mistake is made in the reading of the commentary, the reader merely stops, pauses two seconds (for identification purposes), and starts the sentence again. The mistake is removed on the bench.

The second method is to record the commentary to fit the picture. The commentator should be seated in a soundproof room, from which he can see the picture being projected – soundproof because the projector will be running whilst the recording is being made. He must then be cued in some way, so that he starts particular sections of the commentary in the correct places: pause marks will be indicated in the written script, and the commentator will restart on the next given cue.

The usual methods of cueing are by footage or by marks on the film. For cueing by footage, the commentary must be timed, and the length of each section of commentary known. The commentary is then cued so that sections start at specific footages in the film, and the commentator starts each section of commentary when the appropriate footage is displayed on the footage counter – which, incidentally, should be large and clearly visible in reduced light. It is best for the commentator to be cued by a third person, rather than to have to watch out for the footage numbers himself: a tap on the shoulder, or a flashing light may serve to indicate the start of each section. This is especially true of the other main methods of cueing, from marks on the film itself. Cue-marks which appear on the film itself should be made over several frames, in order to give the commentator time to react to them, and subsequently to start in a natural and unhurried style.

With commentary and all studio recordings, care must be taken to avoid extraneous noise during takes. Chairs must not be scraped, clothes should not rustle, and the cueing assistant must not cough or breathe too heavily. The commentator must be careful of his script sheets: they should be separate, not pinned together, and clearly typed, on one side only, and in double spacing. If the corners of the sheets are turned up, they may be easier to move quietly to one side when finished. If sheets are angled up from the table top, the commentator will not have to drop his head as he reaches the bottom of a page, and will consequently keep a better view of the picture.

Unless very sophisticated recording equipment is used, mistakes made when recording to picture cannot be rectified by merely running back to the beginning of the section, or synchronization between picture and commentary will be lost. If a mistake is made it is best to carry on as normal, and re-record the fluffed sentence at the end of the tape. All such retakes must be separately announced on the tape, and great care must be taken to ensure that timing, acoustics and recording levels are exactly the same as the main part of the tape, or the retakes will be instantly noticeable when cut into the sound-track. The retake is cut into the main track on the bench during track-laying.

Big recording studios and specially equipped sound labs (which frequently offer commentary recording as one of their standard services) usually have recording equipment of the 'roll-back' or 'rock and roll' type, where recording medium and picture are locked in sync, and both can be run back to any necessary point and sections recorded again where mistakes have been made.

A few more general points should be noted about commentary recording: when recording commentary, careful logging of all reels is essential; after the recording session, go through all takes with the commentator – fluffs missed first time round may be noticed, and the commentator may wish to improve intonation etc. in some passages; always rehearse before taking, to enable the commentator to settle down and to establish the pace, and so that the recording levels can be established; nevertheless, always record the rehearsal run – it may possibly have a spontaneity that will elude later takes and, if it does go well, so much the better. Nothing is lost if nothing comes of it. The tape can always be used again.

MUSIC

Large-scale orchestral recordings to pictures are the province of the feature film, but most film-makers will find that they will record their own music of some kind, be it only a piano, guitar, solo nose-flute or small group. The technique of recording music is very elaborate, and each situation requires much care and thoroughness to provide the best quality in recording. The best criterion of successful music recording is how it sounds, and the achievement of optimum sound comes through experiment, trial and error. Musical instruments differ radically in their acoustic characteristics, and recording locations vary equally, so the only advice that can be followed is that of the sound recordist's ears. A few general guidelines may, however, be suggested.

A ribbon microphone, with its particular sensitivity, is usually very suitable for music recording; and assuming that the acoustics of the recording location are reasonably good (or have been suitably adapted), it is better to use one microphone at a distance than to have two or more placed close up. Close placing of several microphones will lead to problems in re-constituting a balanced sound in the actual recording.

Stringed instruments, especially in their higher frequency range, tend to produce very directional sound, radiating in a narrow angle perpendicularly out from the sound board. By placing the microphone away from the direct perpendicular path of the high frequencies, it may be possible to accentuate the lower frequencies (bass) of the sound.

Wind instruments are not so critical: microphone placings above or in front of the player will often be found to produce good results. Again, experiment will indicate the best placing. With all instruments, beware of unwanted mechanical sounds, which can easily be picked up if the microphone is placed too close: the operation of keys and valves on wind instruments, or the scraping of bows and fingers on strings, can easily figure on the music recording if care is not taken.

Recording a piano depends very much on the acoustic nature of the location, and the type of piano. With a grand piano, a good place to start tests is perpendicularly out from the sound-board. Moving the microphone to the tail of the piano will tend to reduce the bass content of the sound, while moving it towards the keyboard will increase bass. With an upright piano, start directly behind the piano, or, if the lid is open, near the pianist's right shoulder. As with all music recording, make as many trial recordings as possible, and listen to the sound of each carefully. With music recording, each situation and each instrument is a different proposition. Care in recording is repaid by the quality of the sound finally available for the film.

Library music – choice and recording

For musical recordings which are beyond the live recording scope of most small-unit productions, the many film music libraries are invaluable. These libraries have a wide selection of music specially written for film use, covering a wide range of tempos, moods, rhythms and musical styles. All libraries supply catalogues of their music (listed both alphabetically by titles, and also according to the type of music) and disks from which to choose the music. A library of these disks will probably be built up by most small film units; alternatively, the libraries have listening facilities where film-makers can hear and select tracks.

When the music has been selected and timed, apply to the library for the tape recording of the track concerned, which can be supplied in varying speeds and track layouts. From these tapes transfers are made to 16-mm. magnetic film in the normal way, and the music is laid into tracks.

The next step is to obtain a licence from the Mechanical-Copyright Protection Society Ltd,★ to which all libraries are affiliated, and which handles copyright licences for all of them. The fee for this licence will be based upon the use of the film, the use of music in the film, and the duration of the music required, the charges normally being made for time-units of 30 seconds. Full details of charges and categories of prospective film usage (commercial, educational, instructional) and distribution (Britain, Europe, world) which affect licence fees, can be obtained from MCPS or any of the music libraries.

★ In the USA, the licence is obtained from the Harry Fox Agency, 110 East 59th Street, New York, NY 10022.

EFFECTS

The sound effects required to stimulate the sound-track of non-sync films or sequences will partly be noted in the film script, and, probably, partly listed by the sound editor when he is laying the tracks. The effects track is of very great importance to the over-all effect of the sound-track, and will probably be revised and added to most of the time that the sound-track is being compiled. The editor himself will develop a feel for when effect is needed, and when it is better left out. The recordist's job is to find and record an effect that is suitable for the purpose: most effects will be post-recorded and post-synchronized.

Sound effects are of two broad types: background or atmospheric effects, and spot effects, which relate to a particular on-screen action. Generally there will be no basic difference in recording for the two types of effect, except that spot effects will have to be more closely tied to the length of action on screen: for instance if a background sea effect is needed, the recordist can shoot an ample footage of the effect, and the editor will then cut it to length on the bench. If, however, a spot effect of a referee blowing a whistle is required, for the best effect the whistle recorded should be of the length required by the picture. Theoretically, a section of a longer whistle could be used, but this may well lose the characteristic sharpness and pattern of the sound required.

Spot effects, particularly, should be carefully studied before recording, to establish the best way to shoot the effect. Different microphone positions can be tried, and the best used; and in doubtful cases (since it is usually impossible to see the film while recording the effect), several different versions should be taken. With spot effects, it is important to get the microphone close to the sound source, eliminating as much ambient noise as possible. A microphone is non-selective, in contrast to the ear and the brain, and a recorded sound can be very different from a natural sound. In some cases it may be found that even after every possible alternative has been tried, the recorded sound is not even approximately right when put to the relevant picture; or that, however close the microphone has been placed to the sound source, there is still an unacceptable amount of extraneous noise on the recording. In such cases, the effect will have to be faked, and the ingenuity of the sound recordist is called into play. A notorious example is that of trying to record a gunshot: when actually recording, it is very difficult to arrive at a result which sounds anything like a gun when played back, and faking in any one of a number of obvious ways is far more convincing on film than the real thing. Almost all effects can be faked somehow, and it is surprising how often the fake turns out to sound more lifelike than the actual recording. One further point about the recording of spot effects: sound effects, like picture takes, can be broadly divided into long-shots, medium-shots and close-ups. Care should be taken that if the picture is close-up, the sound effect should be recorded in close-up too, and vice versa. However, there is a certain latitude in this rule, since certain conventions about the audibility of dialogue and effects have grown up with the cinema: two cowpokes riding the trail in MLS can quite legitimately be heard conversing over distances from which, in 'real' terms, even healthy yells would be faint. Here again, it is a question of assessing the needs of the particular scene.

Recording background effects is normally quite straightforward: decide how obtrusive or unobtrusive the background effects need to be, and record them in a suitable manner. Sharp, identifiable sounds in the background will draw attention to it, and should be avoided for ordinary general effects. This point must also be specially borne in mind when recording for loops. Loops are frequently used when sections of background effects are needed – say street and traffic effects; they comprise one length of effect, say 10 ft, which is joined end to end, and laced up to repeat endlessly, being faded in and out during the dubbing, as needed. When recording for a loop, it is most important that any strong or noticeable sounds are avoided: if such a sound is in a loop, it will be repeated every 10 ft, and will be apparent to the audience.

Finally, with regard to effects recording, the question of 'fill' takes should be noted. 'Fill', 'shush' or 'buzz' is the barely audible background noise that is used to fill in parts of the sound-track where no other sound is being used. Cutting out all recorded sound, and filling in the track with spare picture film, results in very noticeable 'drop-out' on the final sound-track. Unmodulated magnetic film can be used to fill in gaps, but it is better to have specially recorded 'shush', which can vary slightly according to the scene: it can be recorded – with the record level turned right down, exterior or interior, and in a number of different situations.

'Shush' takes should always be carefully announced on the tape, and marked on the tape box, as they may otherwise get mislaid or recorded over by mistake.

RECORDING WITH SYNC SOUND

When the sound is being recorded in synchronization with the picture, all the above remarks will apply, except, obviously, those about post-recording and faking effects: the quality of the sound recording will remain dependent upon the same factors whether or not the tape recorder is linked to the picture. There are one or two extra points to bear in mind, though most are purely mechanical factors involved with the physical operation of the equipment. To keep the microphone correctly placed, it may be necessary to follow the movements of characters or objects. This can be done by hanging the microphone on a boom, or by concealing several microphones near the various points of the movements. Such movements, however made, will have to be rehearsed, to ensure that a constant sound level is achieved, that the boom operator, if used, does not interfere with the lighting, or any other aspects of the technical set-up, and that the boom or microphone (or their shadows) do not appear in the picture.

Another method of following sound in sync shooting is to record by means of a highly directional cardioid microphone – a rifle or a parabolic reflector microphone – mounted on a tripod near the camera, and swivelled to remain pointing towards the main sound source. This set-up is especially useful for hurried location work, or other situations where rehearsal is not possible; it is also a good way of covering very long movements, and sound in extreme long-shots, when some detail is required.

With any kind of microphone, it is important that it should be kept at least 3 ft away from even a well-blimped camera: camera-motor sounds are all too easily picked up on sync sound-tracks. If the microphone has to be close to the camera, as with big close-ups, an answer may be to use a directional mike, and keep a dead side towards the camera. This will have to be checked, however, in the light of the situation in which the recording is being made.

11 The laboratories

Every film will require the services of film laboratories at some stage or other, and it is important to know exactly what services are available and how to go about making the best use of them. Laboratories, in fact, will provide or arrange for every job needed in connection with making a film: in theory the only tool one needs to make a film is a cheque book, and the only location necessary is an armchair by the telephone. From the script right through to the finished print – shooting, editing, track-laying, mixing – every process can be arranged. Thus it should first be asked, to what extent does the film-maker want – or to what extent can he afford – the laboratory to be involved in the film? To answer this, the film-maker must consider the services individually, and measure the facilities he has available himself, including finance. Laboratory facilities can be classed in two sections: essentials, and useful services. The essentials are jobs that virtually all film units of any kind will send to the labs, such as processing and printing; the useful services, such as master assembly and titling, are jobs that may be beyond the scope of small units, or, in large units, are most efficiently organized by subcontracting to labs.

Laboratory work is probably best discussed in two areas: the processes concerned with the picture, and the work of the dubbing theatre on the sound-track.

Essential services carried out by the labs in connection with the picture film are: processing; rush printing; final printing, including grading and colour correction; optical printing, including reduction printing and special effects; preparation and printing of optical sound-track; application of magnetic stripe to print; waxing, scratch treatment etc.; preparation of duplicate masters. Other frequently used services – though many small film units will carry them out themselves – include: negative (or reversal master) cutting, matching master to cutting-copy; titling and other rostrum camera work; preparation of title and subtitle cards; master examination and report.

Other services, such as picture cutting and selection of takes, track-laying and selection of music, script-writing, commentary recording, hiring personnel – in fact, any or all of the tasks of film-making – can be specially arranged.

The essential services are the functions that virtually no film unit, however well equipped, will be in a position to carry out themselves. The expense, size and complexity of the necessary machines render them an impractical proposition for the amount of work they would be required to do for a single unit; even the big feature film production companies invariably have all processing done by independent labs.

Laboratories have full experience of processing every type of filmstock, and have facilities for all kinds of specialized processing. However, many labs do not handle every kind of processing, especially with colour stocks. It may be found that one lab offers processing of Ektachrome films, but will not handle Gevachrome, while the labs equipped for Gevachrome processing may not have facilities for Eastmancolor. Kodachrome processing, particularly, is a protected operation, and can only be provided by the Kodak processing labs. It is therefore important, when using colour stock, to ensure that the labs chosen have the facilities to handle the stock used; although most firms will subcontract work that they are unable to handle, it will be quicker to go direct to an appropriate laboratory. Similarly, some labs may subcontract optical and special-effects printing or other work, and so it is necessary to contact a laboratory before sending work to them. Get a catalogue of their services and prices, talk, or write, to the general manager of the lab, and the head of the department in question, and ask for any special instructions for preparation of work, and for details of their service. Establishing all aspects of lab procedure before dispatch of work will save valuable time and worry during the processing of the film.

Processing by laboratories should not take long: if there is a lab within delivery distance it should be possible to get overnight service for processing and supplying of rush prints. For film units operating outside the delivery distance of a suitable lab, service is normally by return of post.

When the final print is to be made and processed, lab machinery and expertise is needed again. Grading and colour correction (see p. 144) will need to be assessed, and the experience of the lab's specialist grader will be called on. A close contact between the film-maker and the lab at this stage is obviously desirable, particularly if there are any considerations in the grading which are not immediately obvious. If possible, the film-maker should be present at the labs for a grading conference, where details are discussed with the grader. Full instructions as to the appearance of the final print, the rescuing of poorly exposed material, or any special grading effects should be given, otherwise the grader will grade the master to produce as consistent a print as possible, both in exposure and (when applicable) colour.

The preparation of an optical master sound-track is another process which is exclusively carried out in the labs. Once again, close contact with the labs is important, especially if the optical master is to be produced at a different place from that at which the picture is to be printed. In this case, care must be taken that the optical master is negative or positive, as required, for printing with the action master, and that the sync arrangements are clearly understood.

Virtually all opticals and special effects are produced at the labs, although it is possible to effect fades and dissolves in certain cameras, and matte boxes do allow a number of effects to be made during shooting. All opticals, however, are far better produced at the editing and printing stages, when their exact position and duration can be decided in the context of the whole film. In 16-mm. work, with A and B Roll assembly of master material, fades and mixes can be produced during the actual printing of the film, by manipulation of the printer light. However, more elaborate opticals – freezes, wipes, reverse printing etc., as well as dissolves for single-roll master assembly – must be done on an optical printer.

First it should be ascertained whether the lab can actually carry out the optical printing required – again it may be found that some labs subcontract, possibly adding to the cost of the film – and then a list of available effects and their prices should be obtained. Different labs may offer different effects: for example, the range of wipes available may vary from lab to lab. Most labs charge a setting-up fee for all optical printing, a basic charge made before any of the footage charge; so a single freeze-frame, for example, may prove to be relatively costly. For this reason, all optical printing should be done at one time: the editor should not send off for any such work until he knows that he has all the optical printing for the film together.

Several other services are almost always carried out by the labs. The cleaning of the master material and treatment of it for scratches or other defects is sometimes necessary before printing in order to get the best-quality print. The finished print may be given permafilm treatment, or waxed. For magnetic sound copies, a magnetic stripe and balancing stripe will need to be applied to the film, and though machines for applying laminated stripe to films are available fairly cheaply, the quality of stripe applied accurately in the labs is inevitably superior. Duplicate masters and internegatives, for printing large numbers of copies of a film, or simply to safeguard valuable original masters, are also made by the processing laboratory.

Further lab services which are perhaps more usually carried out by the film unit itself, especially on a small budget, may be classed as useful rather than essential. Hiring of personnel for script-writing, camerawork, editing etc., will probably not be contemplated by a small-budget film unit, but services such as matching master material to the cutting-copy, negative cutting and assembly, commentary recording to picture, making up title cards, rostrum camerawork and other work of a similar nature may prove useful and even economic where unit facilities are limited.

Apart from the essential lab services, it is for the film-maker to assess the needs of the film, the finance, the facilities and staff available, and accordingly to decide how far he will employ laboratory assistance. Once this is decided, and the laboratory chosen, he should find out how that particular lab likes to have work presented. Many points are standard, but not all, and presenting work to a lab in a suitable manner will aid efficient service.

Film sent for processing should be marked with information about filmstock, gauge, emulsion type, reversal or negative, ASA rating of camera exposure, length of roll, any special instructions and, most important, any damage or suspected damage. Film-processing machines run many hundreds of feet of film at the same time; any breakdown in the machine, which might be caused by damaged film-stock, will ruin all this film. Much footage is irreplaceable: compensation for the cost of the raw filmstock will hardly seem adequate to someone who may have spent days carefully shooting a piece of film, only to have it ruined at the labs through someone else's carelessness.

When sending work by post, practical administrative instructions should not be forgotten: sender's order number and/or address for invoice; whether to send or hold the master; the number of prints required; black-and-white or colour cutting-copy; and a telephone number for queries. Where possible, also add the production number of the film, its title and director's name: this is especially important where the master is to be held by the labs.

Camera report sheets, compiled as indicated in Chapter 8, are useful in conveying information about exposed film, and should be sent with the film to the labs. As well as carrying information as outlined above, they will also indicate which takes are to be printed: if only the desired takes are printed, costs will be reduced, and the editor's time will be saved if he does not have to sort through piles of takes the director knows to be no good.

At the approval and release printing stage, accurate preparation of work and clear printing instructions are even more important than at the processing and rush print stage, and as close contact as possible should be kept with the labs during printing. The first thing is to ensure that all the master material is accurately assembled, with opticals clearly marked. Leaders should be of the correct length, and marked up clearly. Sync marks should be checked on all sound and picture rolls, and the frame should have a hole punched through it. Also check the maximum reel length, whether to zero the sync mark or the first frame for footage measurements, and whether winding is required emulsion-in or emulsion-out. The film-maker must know at this stage exactly what he wants from the film, and should pass on his instructions to the labs absolutely clearly. Instructions for printing should include:

production company
production number

title of film

director's name

description of master material (filmstock – gauge, type, neg. or pos. master, and type of assembly – A and B rolls, single roll etc.)

kind of print required (b/w or colour – specify printing stock – mute or sound – optical or magnetic – state sync arrangements)

number of prints, including approval print

grading instructions (it is better to attend a grading conference, but if this is impossible, specify any deviations from the obvious)

full list of fades and mixes required during printing (true opticals will have been executed separately and included in the master)

instruction for magnetic striping if required

instructions for waxing or other treatment of print; and if necessary cleaning of the master

whether to hold or return master after printing

source of any master material not enclosed (e.g. the mixed magnetic sound-track may be forwarded direct from the dubbing studio at a different address)

production company's order or account number

telephone number for queries

An example – though this cannot be necessarily taken as a specimen – of instructions for printing might be as follows:

Electrographic Films. Production No. SP 70/012
From Out of a Box. Director: H. Heywood.

Please supply one graded black-and-white optical sound print on Ilford stock of this film. The magnetic mixed master track will be forwarded to you from X Ltd.: please transfer this to 16-mm. optical negative and print with enclosed A and B Rolls Ilford Mark V negative master, 24 f.p.s., level sync. The following fades and mixes are marked on the master:

006 ft.	fade-in	A roll
024	mix	
129	fade-out	B roll
130	fade-in	A roll
229	mix	
437	mix	
514	fade-out	B roll

Grading: the last shot is deliberately light to allow for super-imposition of black end titles. Note that 303–342 ft. is night-time sequence. Several rather over-exposed shots around 440–470 ft. – can these be printed down?

Please give permafilm treatment to print, and supply reel and can for it. Our order no. SP 5884: please return master with print. In event of any query, please ring the director at 0742–56101.

Any further details should be written into the print order where they are necessary. One of the most important things is to become well acquainted with a particular lab, and use it regularly. It will be useful to both the film-maker and the laboratory to know the people they are dealing with, and for them to know each other's way of working. It is best to continue to use a laboratory suiting the film-maker's requirements, unless, of course, a high standard is not maintained. In any case, the labs are a vital element in the completion of a film, and full use should be made of them.

THE DUBBING STUDIO

The dubbing studio is to the sound-track what the processing labs are to the picture. Many dubbing and sound studios are attached to the processing labs, but this is not always the case.

Although it is quite possible to produce a sound-track for a film without employing a sound studio at all, in point of fact any but the simplest of films needs better results than are obtained by direct recording on to stripe, or separate $\frac{1}{4}$-in. magnetic tape – which are, in fact, the only possible alternative methods to fully laid and mixed tracks, for which the dubbing studio is essential. Some of the processes of the dubbing studio can be done by a moderately well-equipped film unit: transfer from $\frac{1}{4}$-in. tape to 16-mm. film for track-laying can be done via a double-band projector, such as the Siemens 2000. But even if this process is done by the film-maker himself – and the quality is virtually certain to be far inferior to a transfer carried out on expensive dubbing studio machinery – the mixing of the tracks is impossible without a set-up that is beyond the reach of almost all small film units. It is a specialized job, which, moreover, calls for highly specialized and skilled operation. (There is now one exception to this. The Prevost 8-plate editing-table, if fitted with the appropriate accessories, is capable of mixing two magnetic tracks on to one, with very satisfactory sound quality. However, the number of mixes required to produce even a moderately complex sound-track makes this more suitable for trial mixes, or for films that do not have to be produced to the very highest professional standards: where maximum quality is necessary, a proper mixing studio is still necessary.)

The dubbing studio, like the processing labs, will offer a wide range of services, some of which may be classed as essential, others as useful. The essential services are transfer, mixing, and dubbing to magnetic stripe. Useful additional services include track-laying, selection and recording of music and effects, and commentary timing and recording.

As with the processing labs, it is important to contact the dubbing studio before the first lot of work is sent, to establish the studio's way of working, and to obtain instructions for preparation of work. This is especially important, as the effect of the dubbing theatre's work on the sound-track is potentially even greater than that of the processing labs on the picture. In the mixing stage, the dubbing mixer at the studio has total control over all sound levels throughout the track: by varying the balance and relative audibility of certain sections of the sound-track, he can, theoretically, completely alter the effect of the film's sound, and thus of the whole film. Close co-operation between the film-maker and the mixer is thus of paramount importance, if the film is to be completed to the intended pattern.

For all but the very simplest sound-tracks, all recorded sound must be transferred from the original recording medium (usually $\frac{1}{4}$-in. tape) to a suitable magnetic film of the same dimensions as the picture film, in order that the sound-tracks may be laid to the picture in a synchronizer. As noted above, it is possible to carry out this transfer process via some double-head film projectors; however, results obtained by this method are normally only satisfactory when maximum sound quality is for some reason not essential – trial sound-tracks, or exercise or test films. For most film work, the transfer should be carried out on the best professional equipment – Leevers-Rich, Westrex etc. For sync sound, too, it is essential that the transfer be done on the correct equipment. Synchronization is normally kept by an electronic pulse recorded on to the master tape at the time of shooting, which controls the precise speed of the transfer and ensures that the sound on the magnetic film will fit the relevant picture exactly. Sync pulse transfer can only be carried out on the correct equipment, and must be handled by a suitably equipped dubbing studio.

It should be remembered, moreover, that during the compilation of the sound-track the actual sound will be transferred at least three times (see p. 88), and each of these transfers is bound to involve a slight loss of quality, so it is best to minimize this loss by always using the best-quality machinery. Besides, transfer to magnetic film is not expensive and the cost of the magnetic film itself must be borne, even if the transfer is done by the film unit on a double-head projector.

Sound for transfer should be sent or delivered to the studio with a full description of the recording techniques employed and with all details of the transfer desired. The description of the recording should include:

whether it is sync or wild (if sync, note the pulse rate – 50 or 60 cycles)
the type of recorder used
full-track or half-track recording
running speed of recording
any special circumstances relating to the recording
administrative notes (production company and number, recordist's and director's name, title of film, tape roll number, production company's order number, and date)

A sound report sheet will include these details, and will enable the director to indicate which sound takes he wants transferred: as with the picture, time and money will be saved by not transferring takes known to be no good (NG).

Instructions about the kind of transfer required will indicate:

the gauge of the film

centre-track or edge-track: on 16-mm. magnetic film, the recording does not cover the entire width of the film, but is situated either in a band along the edge of the film, or along its centre; most editing equipment will handle both, but if the equipment to be used will only accommodate one, be sure that the right disposition of transfer is chosen. Where there is a choice, the centre-track is normally chosen, as the area recorded is slightly wider than with the edge-track – 0·012 in. as opposed to 0·010

running speed of transfer – 24 or 25 f.p.s.

send or hold master

address for delivery of the rushes

The sound studio may provide special labels, with space for all necessary information. If this is the case, these should be obtained before shooting, and fixed to the tape boxes when they are sent for transfer.

The *mixing* of two or more laid magnetic tracks into a final mixed master, suitable for dubbing to magnetic stripe or converting to optical master for printing with the picture, is almost always carried out in the dubbing studio. As indicated above, the contribution of the dubbing mixer to the final sound-track is crucial. It is therefore imperative that he be given very clear instructions for the mix. The director and editor should always be present at a dubbing session. A cue sheet can, at best, only give bald information, which may need amplification for best results in the mixing. Furthermore, the dubbing mixer's experience may suggest some small refinements, and a director or editor should be there to sanction such ideas, or to reiterate the original idea behind the passage. The layout of the dubbing chart may be important: some studios work from a horizontal dubbing chart, others from a vertical pattern, so the blanks supplied by the chosen studio should always be used. In addition, all tracks should be laid as far as possible. Although loops will often be used – for background effects for example – it is unwise to compose a major music track from disks cued in on the dubbing chart: a laid music track will be more reliable, especially when the film-maker is not present for the mix.

Above all, anything unusual or special should be clearly described. The same sound in the same place in the same film can have a different effect according to the way it is used and its relationship with the sound around it, and the mixer must know which effect the film-maker wants to achieve.

It must always be remembered that the dubbing mixer will be coming completely fresh to the film at the dubbing session, whereas the film-maker will have been in close contact with it over six months or more. Ideas and sounds that seem plain to the person who laid the tracks may appear far from obvious to a man hearing them for the first time.

Before the work is sent to the studio – in fact as soon as track-laying begins – the equipment and layout of the chosen dubbing studio should be reconnoitred, so that the tracks can be laid to take best advantage of those facilities. For example, one well-known studio is equipped with a Westrex rock-and-roll system; five playoff heads, including loops (1×100 ft max.); two-disk playoff; edge-track or centre-track, 24 or 25 f.p.s. (footages can be displayed either 16-mm. or 35-mm.); and a commentary studio showing picture and footages on closed-circuit TV monitors. Using a set-up such as this, you should organize the sound-tracks accordingly. If more than five laid tracks and loops are to be used, some pre-mixing will have to be arranged, the tracks to be pre-mixed selected, and their order established. The size of loops must, obviously, be kept within the limits of the equipment's capacity: if two loops are required concurrently, only one can be of over 10 ft.

Finally, instructions from the studio about the presentation of work should be carefully followed. Making up of leaders (e.g. academy leader with 6-ft spacing ahead), measuring of footage (e.g. zero first frame, or zero sync mark), sync marking (level or offset), and maximum reel length will all be points to be observed. The cutting-copy of the picture, or a 'slash print' (a reversal print taken from a cutting-copy), will also be needed by the mixer, who will mix the tracks to the picture. The film-maker should ensure that his cutting-copy is in good condition, and that the splices are good and strong – double-sided, if using tape joins. And lastly, ensure that all tracks, loops and $\frac{1}{4}$-in. tape (if any) are correctly wound, and that everything is clearly labelled. A telephone number, for any queries during the dubbing session, should also be given to the studio.

When the mixed master magnetic track has been completed, it should be checked against the cutting-copy and script by the director. With as many variables as exist in even a three- or four-track mix, the best dubbing mixer in the world may still not have captured the film-maker's intentions after one or two mixes. A final check, then, must be made before marrying the sound to the picture on a magnetic stripe – which, again, should be done on the best equipment in a dubbing studio, though simpler machinery will produce results – or by means of an optical master.

As with work on the picture, so with the sound-track; labs can be used in capacities other than their essential ones, and functions such as track-laying, commentary recording and music and effects selection and recording, can be done by any dubbing studio. Most film-makers, however, will find that these are tasks that are best done by the film unit: tasks which require the judgment and skill of the film-maker, and which have a deep effect on the final nature of the film. Of course, with certain kinds of film, particularly those with which the makers feel no great involvement, or where – as for example in a straight instructional film – there is little chance of mistaken interpretation of the written script, the film unit may find it convenient or economical to have much of the sound work done by the studios. The choice may well depend on the film's budget and the time available: the equipment necessary for these jobs will probably be available to most film units. It must be remembered, though, that services include bookings of rooms and personnel (track-laying, for example, will include the booking of a cutting-room and a sound editor) and may require advance notice.

With all work involving laboratories, either with sound or picture, the need for close co-operation and clear communication is of the greatest importance. The film-maker and the labs form a vital partnership in the completion of the film, and everything must be done to keep that partnership functioning smoothly.

12 Picture editing

Editing covers all stages between the shooting and recording of the film and the finished print, with the exception of laboratory work. It involves arranging all the material available for making the film, the preparation of this material for printing, and deciding what is to appear in the final print, and the manner in which it is to be presented. Editing controls the entire 'feel' of the film, and in many kinds of film is its most important single stage. In short, it is an enormous and very complex subject, which can be, and has been, treated from many angles, in a series of entire volumes: from Eisenstein's and Pudovkin's influential aesthetic analyses of the twenties, to purely technical instruction manuals such as John Burder's excellent *The Technique of Editing 16-mm. Films*, by way of perhaps the most useful of all to anyone concerned with learning what editing really involves, the second edition of Reisz and Millar's *The Technique of Film Editing*.

The above paragraph, however, is not intended as an exposition of the function and problems of editing. It is meant merely to indicate that to try to describe the editing stages of a film in a single short chapter is almost certain to lead to simplistic and incomplete proposals; to recognize that, in the present context, the aim can only be to suggest problems, and indicate a method of approach.

The function of the editor does vary between different types of production, and according to the size of the film unit. In feature films, there are a number of people involved in the editing stages of the film: a picture editor, with a varying number of assistants, a sound editor and assistant, a dubbing mixer, and various technicians. In a small-budget film, it is likely that one man will perform all functions, and he must combine versatility with specialization. The editor must carry out all tasks, both those calling for mere mechanical manipulation, and those requiring skill and judgment, from synching the rushes to the A and B Roll assembly of the master for printing. One man will probably cut the picture, lay the sound-tracks, and supervise the mixing of the sound and its marrying to the picture. Once the picture and sound are shot, one man will be responsible for the final appearance of the print. When Pudovkin said that 'Editing is the creative force of film reality', he may have been overstating his point, and talking about a particular kind of film, but there are very few films indeed in which the contribution of the editor is not a crucial factor.

There is one resounding generalization to be made about editing, before considering in more detail the stages of putting a film together. That is, that all editing must be carried out meticulously. Shoddiness can have a curious effect. Since the average audience is not aware of precisely what is involved in the editing of a film, the effect of bad editing will be to make the audience feel ill at ease, or bored, even though the story may be inherently interesting, and the camerawork and direction satisfactory. It is often said that good editing should pass unnoticed: this may be a gross over-simplification, but the grain of truth in it is evident. Even if the editing is of a more overt nature, if it is successful it will be the total effect of the film, rather than that of the editing, which comes over. Moreover, good editing is remarkably satisfying to the editor: the pleasure of seeing a cut working really well – or a sound effect or mix – can be quite out of proportion to its actual importance in the film (the editor must, of course, retain his sense of proportion).

To a certain degree, especially in small-unit films, the nature and extent of the editing will differ according to the nature and extent of the script. At one extreme, in a totally scripted industrial or instructional film, the editor may have to follow a pre-arranged script sequence exactly, and his job may be reduced to finding suitable cutting points in the shot material, and then doing the mechanical preparation of the sound-track and master. On the other hand, if the script is imprecise, and the film impressionistic in character, the editor may have very far-reaching decisions to make about the best way of using the available footage: the editor's job, in some cases, may well be equivalent to post-scripting the film.

And the editor is also the film unit's doctor. Part of the editor's job almost always includes a certain amount of making the best of material that, for one reason or another, has not come up to expectations. Occasional poor camerawork or exposure may have to be disguised, or cheated or retaken shots may have to be ordered to overcome a sequence that just won't cut as it was intended; a scene may have to be re-arranged slightly at the editing stage because all the hoped-for footage has not materialized. All the heartache and the thousand natural shocks that film is heir to must be healed in the cutting-room.

EDITING PROCEDURE

Initial stages

When the exposed filmstock is sent to the labs for processing, the editor indicates what kind of cutting-copy he requires. All the initial stages in the editing of a film are done on a rough copy, known as the cutting-copy (usually abbreviated to c/c) or workprint. This is made as a direct ungraded contact print from the camera master, and is used only for editing purposes: by the time the editing is finished, the cutting-copy will be in a pretty rough state. Cutting-copies are of several types: from a black-and-white master, there is no complication – ordinary black-and-white rush prints are supplied. With a colour master, however, it is the usual practice to have black-and-white cutting-copies made, to save costs. For many types of film it is quite satisfactory to cut colour film on a black and white cutting-copy, but there are one or two points to watch. First, black-and-white cutting-copies can be made either on 'blue-sensitive' orthochromatic film, or on panchromatic film, which is slightly more expensive. For most purposes, the blue-sensitive film is adequate, but edge-fogging on the master does not print through. Thus, if there is any suspicion of fogging, the scene must be checked against the master; this will be particularly necessary for shots that occur near the beginning or end of a master roll. Edge-fogging does print through on to a panchromatic film, so for the extra cost, the necessity of checking the master can be avoided.

However, when working with a black-and-white print from a colour master, it is as well to check through the master anyway, in order to assess its colour quality. Sample printing of frames from the colour master, known as 'colour pilots', may be obtained from labs to help with assessment of colour quality, but this is not the usual practice with 16-mm. production. If the budget will stand it, however, it is always useful to have a colour cutting-copy. In most films, the colour itself is a factor which needs taking into consideration during picture editing, and it is almost impossible to remember and visualize colours from looking at a black-and-white cutting-copy.

Have the editing bench ready with the following:

synchronizer	gloves
viewer (if not incorporated in synchronizer)	cans
rewinds	cores
tape splicer	scissors
split spools	chinagraph pencils
trim bin, clip rack or other trim filing system	Gem marker
log book, or sheets	pen or pencil
notepaper	tape

Sort the master from the cutting-copy, and put the master aside, well wrapped and in a can, until it is needed again. The master need not even be opened unless there is some query arising from a glance at the cutting-copy, when it may be necessary to check the master for logging purposes. As mentioned above, fogging does not print through on to a blue-sensitive cutting-copy, and any imperfections on the cutting-copy – for example, processing marks   must be checked against the master to see where the imperfection lies. The cutting-copy will be wound either on a plastic core or on a cardboard centre, in which case it should soon be transferred on to a core. During the editing work, all picture film and sound film is kept on cores: usually 2-in. diameter 'T' cores for lengths up to about 400 ft, and 3-in. 'Z' cores for longer rolls. Cores of 4-in. diameter are also used. The cores fit inside split spools for mounting on rewind arms, or for projecting, and can be removed for storage in cans (obviating the need for a spool for every length of film), or for mounting on the plates of an editing-machine or table.

The first viewing of the cutting-copy is now probably irresistible, even with sync footage which needs its sound synchronized before the rushes can be usefully viewed. A brief run through on an editing machine or through a projector will give some initial idea of the look of the film, and will tell the editor such things as whether all shots are well exposed, whether all the important shots have worked well enough to be used, how much footage there is to work on – and many other general points he will be anxious to know before he starts work. And the first viewing of the rushes will be the editor's first concrete contact with the film: it is the start of his job. The first screening of the rushes is normally the most disappointing time of the entire film, the low point for all who see them – director, cameraman, editor and others. All the shortcomings of the shooting are only too apparent, and none of the solutions provided by editing have yet been found. Retakes, muffed shots, technical errors, missed opportunities are all far more in evidence than the good material that seems to go unnoticed between them. But from this time the editor's mind is working on the film: many of the ideas of the editing may already be suggesting themselves to him, from selection of takes, right down to some individual cuts. The first viewing session can also provide a useful occasion for the director and editor (if they are not the same person) to exchange impressions of the material; as a rule the director should refrain as much as possible from breathing down the editor's neck during the cutting, although close contact must obviously be maintained.

Synchronization of rushes

Where sync sound has been shot, it is clearly essential to have the sound available for projection with the cutting-copy when the rushes are viewed, as it will be impossible to judge the quality and effect of the shooting without listening to the sound as well as looking at the pictures. The sound recorded on $\frac{1}{4}$-in. tape during shooting will have been transferred to 16-mm. magnetic film while the picture was being processed and printed, but since the recorder and camera will

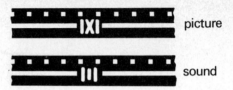

have been frequently stopped and restarted for the different takes during shooting, the picture and sound film will not be in continuous correct synchronization when they return from the labs. The editor's first job, then, will be to cut out the extraneous sound film (since the recorder is always started before the camera, there will always be extra sound), and to bring the sound and picture into sync. The procedure for this is as follows.

Lace two white leaders in the synchronizer (a picture-synchronizer is easier to work with, although a synchronizer and a separate picture viewer can be used together), and attach to two take-up spools on the rewind arms. Mark these leaders, with the Gem marker:

Prod. No. Title 'Action' rushes. Reel 1. Head

Prod. No. Title Sync dialogue. Rushes. Reel 1. Head

After a couple of feet of the white leader, attach a length of good black spacing, and near the beginning of this make a sync mark on each roll, making sure that the marks are on exactly the same frame on each roll. Different marks are used for picture and sound sync and both are preceded and followed by a continuous line for a foot or two, which will assist location of sync marks when winding through quickly. All marks made on the film during editing should be made with chinagraph pencil. Once the sync marks have been made, all joins must be made to the left of the synchronizer.

After about 6 ft of black leader, attach the first picture take to the action roll, including the slate, and run this through the viewer until the strike frame of this first take – i.e. the frame where the arm of the clapper-board first makes contact with the top of the board – is located, and mark the frame with a chinagraph pencil. Next, thread the sound film into the third way of the synchronizer, and run it over the sound head (check that this is set for edge-track or centre-track, as appropriate) until the announcement of the first slate is heard, followed by the sound of the clapper strike. Mark the first frame of this strike with the chinagraph, and place it in sync with the picture strike frame, keeping the sound in the third channel, and wind both back to the point where the picture is joined to the leader. At this point, mark the leader of the sound roll, remove the sound from the third channel, cut it at the mark, and join it to the sound roll leader at the place marked. If possible, the slate announcement should be kept on the sound roll at this stage.

Now wind both sound and picture through together, to check that the strike frame on picture and sound coincide, and then wind both rolls right through together, keeping an eye on the sync.

At the end of the shot, the procedure should be repeated; there should be enough extra sound film to allow it to be doubled back into the third channel of the synchronizer without being cut. The sound trims – those portions of sound film removed during this process – should be carefully rolled, the ends stuck down with tape, marked with their slate and take number, and stored in clearly labelled cans. Some of these sound trims may be quite long, and may contain usable sound; none should be thrown away before a mixed master of the sound-track has been made, and the editor should be able to put his hand immediately on any trim he wants. Rummaging through a large bin full of long and short bits of unmarked magnetic film looking for one trim that has turned out to be necessary after all, is far more time-consuming than the extra effort needed to file all trims neatly during synching of rushes. And remember that magnetic film cannot be identified merely by holding it up to the light: clear marking of all magnetic film trims (and this applies to all stages of editing) will save time and awkward manipulations of the synchronizer.

Continue working as for the first shot, until all takes are synchronized, or until the rolls of film become too large to handle conveniently, when another roll must be started. At the end of each roll of film and sound film, a length of black spacing should be attached, followed by a couple of feet of white leader, bearing the same information as the head leader with the obvious exception that the word 'head' will be replaced by the word 'tail'.

Notes

1 A tape splicer is much more convenient for picture splicing, and is essential for splicing the sound film.
2 Always use the straight cut of the splicer for cuts in the picture. This cuts along the frame line, and avoids the loss of frames when re-making splices.

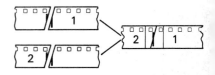

Splicing magnetic film.

3 Always use the diagonal cut of the splicer when cutting magnetic film; this aids the smooth flow of film over the sound heads, and distortion is kept to a minimum. It also avoids a click as the splice passes over the head: in effect a diagonal splice provides a very short sound mix.
4 A method to ensure accurate joining of magnetic film is to use a vertical line on the frame line as a mark; if the join is made correctly, the marks on both pieces of film will reconstitute a whole line:
5 If, at the picture strike frame, there is a frame where the clapper arm is blurred and virtually in the closed position, it is better to use this frame as the strike frame rather than the next, where the clapper will be clearly in the closed position.

6 For the sound strike frame choose the frame in which the sound starts, even if the sound covers only a small part of that frame.

Logging

With the rushes synchronized and given a preliminary screening, the next stage is to log all details of the available material. If specially prepared sheets are not available for this, a book should be prepared with various columns, to record at least the following details of every shot:

Slate no.	Script no.	Action	Dialogue	Edge no.	Remarks
84 Take 1	37	CU Alun, slow pull back as lines spoken, to include R. who beats drum	Such loving... ...rarely loved.	947213 –242	Cam. movement doesn't tie too well with lines. Slightly underex., too.
84 Take 2	37	do.	R. books at 'they loved...'	242– 249	NG
84 Take 3	37	do.	As Take 1	249– 276	OK but final framing rather weak and slight jerk in zoom.
84 Take 4	37	do.	do.	276– 301	Zoom matches lines much better; framing OK.
84 Take 5	37	do.	do.	301– 330	Movement and framing OK – J. moves rather awkwardly: perhaps not as good as t.4

Slate number. With unslated material (though cameramen should be encouraged to slate all material, whether wild or sync, wherever possible), a slate number should be allocated at this point, and written on the film in chinagraph.

Script number. If all shots have a script number, indicating the order in which the shots are intended, assembly is considerably simplified.

Action details, including take-to-take variations.

Dialogue details, noting variations, mistakes etc.

Edge numbers of beginning and end of each shot.

Any remarks about the shot which will help when takes are selected, and when the shots are put in order.

Thorough logging is really worth while: the appropriate paperwork at this stage of a film pays great dividends later. The logging sheets will help in locating shots for use, selecting possible additional shots, cutaways etc., locating shots in the master when the time comes for master assembly, keeping a record of what is in the film and what is not, and for making all kinds of decisions about the general editing patterns of the film – all without having to wind back and forth through a disorganized cutting-copy.

Another important aspect of preparatory paperwork is the transcription of all unscripted dialogue of any kind. The most obvious instance of this will be the live interview, whether recorded sync with a picture, or just taped without a picture, to use as voiceover. There can obviously be no record in the film's script of what is said in such interviews, so the editor must sit down with a tape recorder, and write out on paper the exact words used, making, in addition, notes about the quality of the recording and the suitability of the subject-matter for the purposes envisaged. Transcription can be a fairly tedious task, but, as with all kinds of logging of material, it will repay the effort several times. Editing and selecting an interview on paper is a far easier job than winding through miles of film or tape, and because it is physically easier, the mind can devote all its efforts to the real problems involved, the problems of what is said, and how it relates to the over-all pattern of the sequence of the film.

Selection of takes

When the cutting-copy is logged and synchronized, the editor and director will look at the entire rushes in order to decide which takes should go forward into the rough assembly of the film. Many of the easier decisions will have been taken during the logging: all NG takes, for instance, will be obvious, and the choice between alternative takes may already have been reduced to two or three. Many of the deciding factors between takes will have become clear by this stage: the editor is already familiar with the material, and less obvious aspects of each take are already becoming apparent. The editor and director will need to consider all aspects of the shot: the pattern of movement; whether the subject-matter is satisfactory or not; the quality of the sound recording, and its freedom from extraneous noise; the appropriateness of the camera movements and the framing of the shots; the technical picture quality; possible cutting points; lighting and exposure; interpretation of dialogue, if any – these, and many more such questions, will present themselves as the best takes are selected. If, after careful thought, the right choice is not apparent, both takes should be earmarked for inclusion in the first assembly, and the final choice deferred until more detailed work has been done on the construction of the film, and new factors have arisen to influence the choice. Otherwise, the selected takes can be marked by ringing the slate number on the log sheet, or by some similar means.

Breakdown

Next, all takes must be separated, and hung up on the clip rack, pin rack or whatever film filing system is used. As far as possible, shots should be hung up in script order, and wanted takes can be separated from unwanted ones. With sync tracks, the sound should always be hung up with its related picture, but it is very important to ensure that each shot has a clear sync mark on both picture and sound. Unwanted takes can be rolled up, picture and sound together, if sync, and stored in clearly labelled cans. It is unwise to commit any but irredeemably useless shots to the waste-bin at this stage. In many films there will be too much material to hang up all at once; in this case the film can be broken down, and then assembled in convenient sections. At this stage of a film it is probably better to be working with several small rolls than one or two large, cumbersome ones. Be quite sure to label all the film and cans clearly: it is all too easy to mislay shots or parts of shots when the film is in many little bits. And although clinical cleanliness is not absolutely essential to an editor, a modicum of organization and method is an invaluable help. Finally, it is worth stressing that a breakdown is almost always worth while and advantageous. Especially in very short films, it can seem tempting to leave the rush print in one piece, and proceed with the cutting from there. But, unless the editor is extraordinarily lucky, every shot will have to be cut at both ends anyway, so he might as well save himself a lot of the time and energy used in winding backwards and forwards trying to organize the structure of the sequence. Another case, in fact, of good preparation paying handsome dividends.

Assembly

The cutting-copy is now ready for its first rough assembly. The takes selected are brought down from the clip rack, and are joined in script order, end to end, into as many reels as are necessary and convenient. If sync sound is being assembled, the two rolls, picture and sound, are assembled together, care being taken to see that all sync marks are kept aligned as the shots are assembled. With picture-only assembly all shots are simply spliced end to end. At this stage, it is best not to attempt to cut any of the shots at all – even slate numbers and announcements will be left on in the first instance. The first assembly simply sorts the shots into the right order. Continue assembling all takes until the film – or the sequence – is together, on rolls, and with its sound, if there is any at this stage. Now the film will be ready for its first viewing: either on an editing-machine capable of replaying separate sound, or else via a double-head projector, when picture and sound may be seen together, under conditions of projection.

The rough cut

The editor must now begin making his decisions. He is starting to work on the creative editing process and the decisions he makes at these stages of editing will be those that are most important to the final shape and quality of the film. The first job in the rough cut will be to cut out slates and take announcements, leaving plenty of sync marks on the remaining film, since once the clapper strike is out of the picture and sound, re-aligning lost sync can often be tricky. With the slates out, the editor can begin to see the film flow, and will begin making decisions about re-positioning shots and possibly sequences, about the length of the shots used and which sections of available shots should be kept in, about how to cover up for shots or sequences that have not turned out as envisaged, or have been badly shot, about intercutting, about 'montages' (using this much abused word in its American rather than its Russian sense), and about all the various aspects of the shot material and script which need working on to produce the desired result. Many short films will give the editor considerable scope in constructing the rough cut of the film. Especially if the director and script-writer is also editing the picture, many of the actual decisions about the basic nature of the film may even be left until the rough-cut stage of editing.

In more formally scripted films, and ones where the editor is not otherwise involved in the creation of the film, the editor may well still have many very significant decisions and choices to make. Dialogue scenes, or scenes strictly related to a commentary, may perhaps have little scope for the editor beyond getting the shots in the right order, organizing intercutting and choosing the cutting point; but, for example, with an impressionistic montage, the editor will be forced to impose, at least in part, his own visual structure on the film. The director and cameraman will, perhaps, go off and shoot a selection of shots to represent the passing of a season in the country. They will bring back a selection of, say, twenty or thirty shots to cover a thirty-second sequence, and, since this kind of sequence is an open invitation to a cameraman's virtuosity, the editor will probably find that all but two or three of the shots are beautiful and usable. The editor's choice of shots, their number, the pace of their editing, and their juxtaposition, together with the relationship of the chosen shots to the sound-track, will all leave a very distinctive mark on the film.

In fact, scenes that are apparently more regimented – with full scripts, dialogue sequences, and commentary scenes – still depend on the editor to achieve their full effect. Dialogue scenes, to take one example, will probably be shot with plenty of cutaway shots, reaction shots and incident material to give the editor some choice in how to cut the scene together. A speech by one person will not only contain shots of that person speaking, but also shots of the listeners reacting to his words, CU details of the speaker other than his face (hands, dress etc.), objects referred to in his speech, or other surrounding objects of significance – a whole number of extra things which will illuminate or comment upon the main action of the scene.

A further example: a traditional way of shooting a dialogue, in features, is to film all one character's lines in CU first, then all the other person's words in CU, from the viewpoint of the first speaker, and then to shoot the whole conversation again in LS or MS – or both. In either of these examples, the editor is presented with plenty of material, of which he can only use a certain amount, and which offers an enormous range of possibilities in the presentation of the scene. It is the editor's job to cut the scene together, and how he does so will affect the tenor of the sequence.

Of course there are many standard methods of cutting set-piece scenes – Joseph V. Mascelli's *The Five C's of Cinematography* is packed with illustrations of ways in which these have traditionally been done. Better still, Reisz's *The Technique of Film Editing* discusses many aspects of the aesthetic and cinematic side of editing. There is so much about editing which cannot be covered in a description of this nature, that it is important to do further background reading when approaching the task of cutting film for the first time. Even the most experienced editors are continually learning more about their craft.

The rough cut then continues: the final order of shots, the final selection between all alternative takes, the pace of the editing, the cutting of the sync track, if any, and the broad construction of the other sound-tracks, the approximate lengths of the individual shots, the cutting points from one shot to another, the use of opticals and special effects – these and many more decisions must now be made. While working on the cutting of the film, the editor uses a number of standard markings, made on the film with a chinagraph pencil, to indicate ideas that cannot be put into effect until the print stage of the film. These marks will not only remind him of his intentions when he comes to cut the master, but will also tell any other people working on or looking at the cutting-copy what the editor wants – for example if the sound-tracks are being laid to the cutting-copy by a specialist sound editor who has not been involved in cutting the picture, or if a sequence has been passed on to an assistant editor. In all cases, intentions must be clearly and recognizably marked. The following signs are used:

Standard editor's markings.

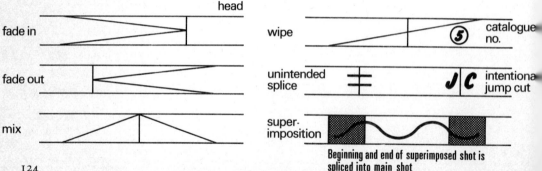

Beginning and end of superimposed shot is spliced into main shot

Where other special effects and opticals are needed, they can be indicated by splicing in a section of marked black leader, until the optical has been produced and a cutting-copy of it is available.

SOME GENERAL NOTES

It is important to develop the ability to see a shot in its sequence, and the sequence in the film: that is to say, the *structure* of the film should always be kept in sight during the editing. One of the prime problems of film-making is the structuring of time, and for this, the part must always be considered in relation to the whole.

Most sequences hang on a *key shot* – a shot to which all before it leads up and from which all after it comes down. There may, of course, be more than one such shot. Identify these shots and structure the scene round them.

All editing depends on *rhythm*: the rhythm of the movement within the shot, the rhythm of the cutting of the shot, the rhythm of the sequence. But the rhythm of film-editing is very difficult to describe in words: it is something that must be felt, and a feeling for it is acquired through experience and thought, combined with innate sensitivity. It is important to note that rhythm in film-editing cannot be achieved by mechanical means: the physical length of the film is not necessarily related to its apparent time on the screen (a static shot will appear far longer on the screen than a shot of identical length which contains subject movement and camera movement). Rhythm is decided through the evidence of the editor's eyes, not through physical measurement. Rhythm also depends on the ability to judge when a particular shot is dead – when its content has been exhausted, and its stay is no longer necessary. A shot outstaying its welcome on the screen will inevitably interrupt the rhythm of the film, by boring the audience, even if only for a fleeting moment. It is often possible to feel visual 'beats' flowing through successful cutting – beats not necessarily regular in time, as in music, but giving the impression of being related one to the other to form a continuing and necessary progression, with no hiatus or slack period.

Develop the ability to *look* at the shots effectively, and actually *see* what is happening on the screen. As with camera-work, it is insufficient to notice merely the main narrative action of the shot: the editor must be able to see the image as a two-dimensional pattern. At cutting points, for instance, the editor often needs to relate the visual structure of the outgoing shot to that of the incoming shot; to do this he will have to choose his cutting point on the basis of two-dimensional information. There may be many cases where a cut looks unpromising if judged only on its narrative content, or even on its main visual content. Skilful appraisal and use of the total two-dimensional image structure may enable an editor to produce an acceptable cut.

Some points to consider while cutting the picture:

Action. A strong action carrying over from one shot to the next will usually provide a good cutting point, but care should be taken to choose the right point in the action for the cut. To place only the first phase of the movement in the outgoing shot, and complete the bulk of the movement in the incoming shot is often successful: this creates expectancy, and fulfils it, and smoothes the cut.

Disposition of highlights. The eye is naturally drawn to the brightest area of the screen, and if this changes in location from one shot to the next, the effect can be distracting. There are many more subtle applications of this principle which can be exploited in cutting. Marking the viewer glass with a chinagraph pencil will aid comparison between two shots.

Balance of compostion. This is clearly a large and complex area, but generally the relation of the composition in the incoming and outgoing shots will be of great importance in making the cut. The editor must know where the audience's eyes will be at the time he makes the cut, and must use this position to take up the action of the next shot – unless he wants to make a deliberate break and force the eye to another part of the screen. Coinciding lines and shapes can help in matching up the balance of the composition; the disposition of highlights will also affect this.

Similarly, the *relationships between the colours* of the two shots, if colour is used, will affect the cut.

Where *dissolves, fades or wipes* are to be used, there must be a similar estimation of the expectancies of the audience's eyes, particularly with dissolves, where both images will be appreciable on the screen together. The wipe is probably a drastic enough transition to cover visual incompatibility between the two shots.

Dialogue, or commentary phrases, may often dictate a cutting point, especially on small-unit films where there may be only one take of the words. The words themselves can sometimes be used to make the cut: the meaning of the word can be related to something visual or verbal at the start of the next shot.

Matching, or opposing, *movements* of a similar kind are frequently useful. This echoing of movement may in fact help the editor to cut together two shots of quite disparate narrative content. In shots of similar or identical content, such matching of movement may contribute to the rhythmic flow of the sequence.

Shock cuts: to build up an atmosphere and a series of expectations in the audience, and then do precisely what is least expected, accompanied by a sharp change in the sound-track, can occasionally be used as a transition from sequence to sequence, or for special purposes, such as horror.

(*Above, left*) Acmade-Miniola editing machine; (*above*) Prevost 6-plate editing table.

A good rule of thumb: if it is difficult to decide whether to include a shot or not, the answer is almost certainly, not. 'If in doubt, take it out.'

By the time the film reaches an advanced rough-cut stage, the final effect of the film will be becoming apparent, to the editor at least. At this stage, an editing-machine – often called 'Moviola' after the brand-name of the most widely used type – is an essential item of equipment. In the early stages of the rough cut, a hand-wound viewer will have been quite adequate for editing purposes, or, if a sync track was to be edited too, a hand-wound picture synchronizer. Now, however, it will be necessary to be able to run the film at a constant and correct speed in order to judge the development of the rhythmic construction of the film, and also the sound of the sync track, if used. There are several types of editing-machine available, the three most widely used in 16-mm. work being the Moviola, the Acmade and the Premier. The Moviola is of a different layout from the other two, but the principle of all of them is the same. A simple projection system displays the picture on a small screen, while the sound, on a separate magnetic film, is run through a separate threading path: the drive sprockets for both picture and sound are locked together in sync, and driven by an electric motor. Controls allow forward and backward running at normal or double speed, and allow the picture to be stopped instantly on any frame. An inching knob allows limited movement for frame-by-frame inspection.

In addition to editing-machines, flat-bed editing-tables exist, such as the Acmade, the Steenbeck and the Prevost. These, as the name implies, are of a horizontal, table-top layout, and run picture and sound separately, in sync, and have instant-stop, inching, reverse running, double speed etc. The advantage of most editing-tables, though, is that they are capable of running two or more sound-tracks simultaneously, so that, when the tracks are being laid, it is possible to judge the effect of two or three tracks at the same time. On what is perhaps the most sophisticated of

Editing bench ready for master assembly.

all these tables, the Prevost 8-plate, there is even provision for mixing sound from two tracks on to a third, so that trial mixes may be made before compiling the dubbing chart.

The fine cut

With the aid of an editing-machine, and/or flat-bed table, the editor will be able to see in some considerable detail what the final film will look and sound like. The progression from the rough to the fine cut of the cutting-copy is continuous and progressive: 'rough cut' and 'fine cut' are relative rather than absolute terms. However, the term 'fine cut' implies something extra: the fine-cut stage is where the final decisions about each cut are made. This is where the editor finally commits himself. The later rough-cut stages will have sorted out the length of the shots, and their positioning, the intercutting, and the interpretation of the sequences. The fine cut now reduces each cut to its exact place. If the rough cut has cut two shots together to the nearest half-dozen frames, the fine cut must decide to the exact frame. There is always one ideal place for the cut: at the fine-cut stage the editor must find this place, and find it for every cut of the film. He must make irrevocable decisions. It is the time when the editor can no longer say, 'I'll think more about that later.'

After the fine cut is completed, the editor's remaining work on the picture is purely mechanical – the preparation of the master for printing in exact accordance with the cutting-copy. In fact, negative cutting services are often hired for this work, though in small film units it is more often the editor himself who is responsible for master assembly. It is essential that it be clearly, accurately and cleanly done.

Master assembly

This begins with logging the edge numbers of the shots finally used in the cutting-copy, and sorting out the relevant takes from the master, which, until now, has remained unopened (except perhaps for initial checks – see above) in its cans. Before opening the cans of the master, ensure that the cutting bench is scrupulously clean, that the trim bins or clip racks to be used are empty and the bags clean, and that anyone who is to handle the film is provided with a pair of soft clean cotton gloves. Master film picks up dust and fingerprints with alarming ease.

Cut all the required takes out of the master, identifying them by the edge numbers, and hang them up in script order. Pre-numbering the film clips will speed this operation. The spare master, left over after required takes have been removed, should be rolled up and put back in cans, and stored out of the way. On each shot used, be sure to leave plenty of extra frames at either end of the required section of a shot, or, preferably, cut the whole shot out of the master, slate and all. Remember that there is no room for a mistake once the master assembly has begun, especially if there is a sync sound-track. Frames lost by careless cutting, or by poorly adjusted splicers, or just by plain boobs, are often very difficult to remedy, and, at the least, will mean a slight alteration in the cutting points of the shot.

When the hanging up is completed, some editors prefer to join all the takes together loosely in script order, and make a roll of the master which can be placed on the rewind arm during assembly, and the shots pulled off in the correct order. Others may prefer to avoid any possible damage due to reeling-up, and leave the film hanging up on the clip racks until needed. Whichever way he chooses, the editor is now ready for the actual assembly.

A and B roll assembly

A 16-mm. master can be assembled all in one roll and printed straight off. In this case, there are no complications in assembly – the shots are simply joined head to tail; the use of a synchronizer will make location of the exact cutting point easier, but it is not essential – the cutting point may be located from the edge numbers on the cutting-copy and the master, with extra frames being counted visually. But there are several drawbacks with printing from a master assembled in one roll. Since, for printing, all joins must be made with a cement splice, which requires an overlap of film, all splice marks will print through onto the final film, and, unless they happen to occur in a dark area of the frame, they will be noticeable on projection. Also, all opticals except fades will have to be produced separately: the master for the optical will have to be sent away to the lab, where the

A and B roll checkerboard assembly.

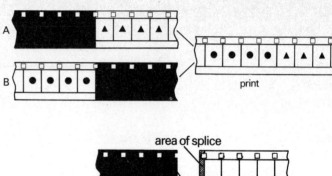

area of splice

black leader cut exactly to frame line

(*Above*) Double-bed 16-mm. frame-line splicer. This is the splicer shown on the bench, p. 128.

(*Right, top*) The result of printing A and B rolls; (*right, lower*) frame-line splice.

effect will be produced on an optical printer; the effect will be included, already completed, in the master for printing. A system known as A and B roll checkerboard assembly has, therefore, been developed, which removes all traces of the splices from the final print, and which allows certain common effects such as the mix to be incorporated in the printing of the film, at considerably less expense than full optical production of the effect. With this method, the master is assembled in two rolls instead of one, each roll containing alternate shots, and filled out for the space of the missing shots with opaque black leader.

These rolls are assembled in exact synchronization, with the joins on both rolls exactly coinciding. Furthermore, all joins are made so that the overlap is covered by black leader, and in addition that overlap reaches exactly to the bottom (or top) edge of the last (or first) frame of the shot. This requires the use of a 'frame-line' splicer (this denotes that the cut and scrape are aligned so as to make the splice area reach the frame line of the shot) with a double bed, enabling the picture to be scraped each time, at the beginning and end of the shot.

When the two rolls are in sync, all splices are covered by black leader, and the first frame of each shot exactly succeeds the last frame of the previous shot, across the rolls.

When this A and B roll checkerboard assembly is complete, the two rolls are printed in succession on to the same piece of raw printing stock. First the A roll is printed, which will print through half the shots and, since the black leader is totally opaque, will leave the gaps between the shots unexposed; the B roll is then printed over this, in exact synchronization. The shots on this roll will now print exactly into the spaces left unexposed after the A roll printing. Since the splices in both rolls occur in the areas covered by black leader, no trace of them will print through on to the final print.

The other chief advatage of A and B roll assembly is that it allows certain opticals to be produced easily and cheaply during printing. Superimpositions, including titles and sub-titles, and dissolves (mixes) are made simply by overlapping

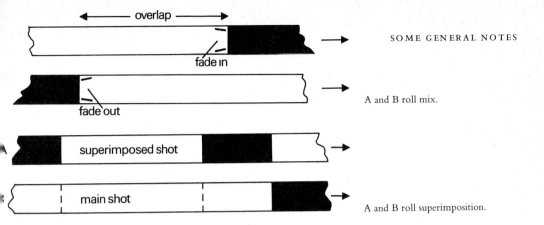

overlap

fade in

fade out

A and B roll mix.

superimposed shot

main shot

A and B roll superimposition.

the picture areas on the two rolls, incorporating fades as necessary, so that the shots print on top of partly exposed film instead of unexposed.

Of course, the assembly need not be limited to A and B rolls only: C, D and E rolls – or more if necessary – can be added on the same principle to cover a range of needs: subtitles, multiple superimpositions and so forth.

The technique of A and B rolling is quite straightforward, but it does often appear to present problems when first attempted, especially as there is no room for errors when assembling the master. Until the technique is completely understood, it is essential to concentrate fully on the task: the kinds of mistake that tend to occur are those which are not easily noticeable – until the final print is seen.

The bench used for A and B roll assembly should be equipped with the following items:

4-way rewind arms
double-bed frame-line splicer
4-way synchronizer
cloth wells on either side of the synchronizer for receiving film
fresh film cement; gloves; scissors; punch; chinagraph pencil; brush (for removing scrapings from splicer)
supply of black leader, equal to the total footage of the film plus a few feet extra

First, thread the final cutting-copy of the film into the third channel of the synchronizer. If the film has a sync sound-track, there will be a sync mark in the leader of the cutting-copy. If so, put this in the zero frame in the synchronizer, and set the footage counter to zero. (Some synchronizers may have the frame counter numbered 1–40 rather than 0–39: in this case set sync mark to 40 and zero the footage counter.) If there is no sync mark, punch a hole in the leader of the cutting copy, exactly 6 ft before the first frame of the first shot of the picture, and place this in the zero frame. Now make up leaders for the master rolls. These will consist of about 3 ft of white leader, followed by black

Example of leader marking the master rolls.

leader; sync marks should be made, and holes punched about one foot in from the start of this black leader, and lined up with the cutting-copy sync mark in the synchronizer. From now on, no roll must be removed from the synchronizer until the reel is completed, and all splicing must be done to the left of the synchronizer. Each roll should be marked, on the white leader, with relevant details – production company, production number, title, filmstock, A or B roll, reel number, and 'head'.

The set-up will now look like this:

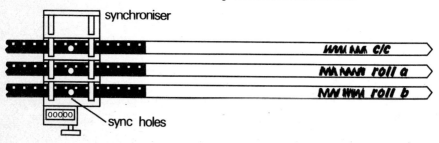

Setting up the A and B rolls and leaders in the synchronizer.

There is often some confusion about which way the emulsion of the master should be facing. If single-perf. stock is used, there is no choice: which emulsion (master or cutting-copy) is up, and which down, will depend entirely on the disposition of the sprockets of the synchronizer. This is not standard: Acmade synchronizers, for example, have sprockets on the side nearer the front of each drum, while Premier synchronizers have the reverse. If, however, double-perf. film is used, and there is a choice, the cutting-copy should be placed emulsion-down, and the master should be assembled emulsion-up. This will minimize the risk of damage to the master.

Now wind the three films through the synchronizer (working, naturally, from left to right) and affix the ends to their respective take-up spools; continue winding until the first frame of the first shot on the cutting-copy is in the synchronizer. Make a mark on the A roll leader, opposite the first frame of the cutting-copy. Wind the film on until the first edge number on the cutting-copy is reached, and mark it. Now take the master for the shot, find the edge number corresponding to the one marked on the cutting-copy, and place it in the fourth channel of the synchronizer, exactly aligned with the same number in the cutting-copy. (Note that edge numbers usually cover the space of two frames; for the marking in this case, take the frame including the last numbers.) With the master and cutting-copy locked in sync, wind all rolls back until the start of the shot is reached and mark this place on the master – take care to make the master mark on the side of the cut that will not be used. Now the mark on the master, the mark on the A roll leader, and the first cut on the cutting-copy will all be in line. Wind the marks back so they are well clear of the synchronizer, cut the master and A roll leader at the marks, and join the master shot to the black leader. At this stage, things will look like this:

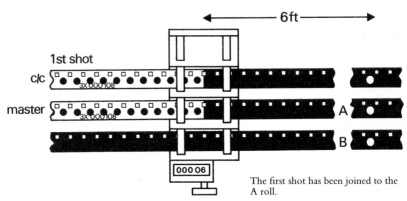

The first shot has been joined to the A roll.

The golden rule of A and B roll assembly is that it is always the picture that is scraped (since the scrape must fit up exactly to the frame line), and never the black leader. This means that the picture always goes to the left-hand side of the splicer, the black leader always to the right. It is easy to slip up on this, especially when the picture is coming off the synchronizer – at the tail of the shot – and it naturally seems to go to the right-hand side of the splicer. This is the time when concentration is essential.

Roll on the synchronizer until the end of the first shot on the cutting-copy is reached. From now on, the procedure will be the same at every cut, apart from slight variation for certain optical effects:

1 Retrieve the master for the following shot. Line up the edge number with the cutting-copy number in the synchronizer, wind back to the beginning of the shot, and mark the cut.
2 Mark the A and B rolls at the cutting point, taking care to mark the unused side of the cut on the master. Remove the new master from the fourth channel.

Five steps in A and B rolling: steps 1 and 2.

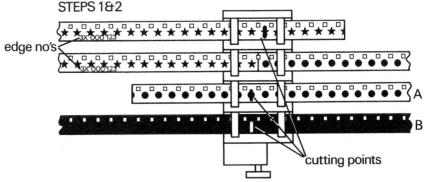

3 Wind all rolls out to the left of the synchronizer. Cut the new master and the A and B rolls at the marked point.

STEP 3

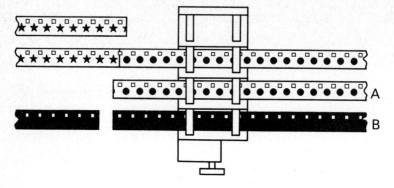

4 Join the tail of the outgoing shot to the black leader, remembering to put the shot in the left-hand side of the splicer, and the black leader in the right.

STEP 4

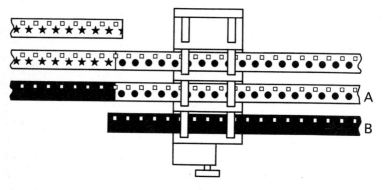

5 Join the head of the incoming shot to the tail of the black leader.

STEP 5

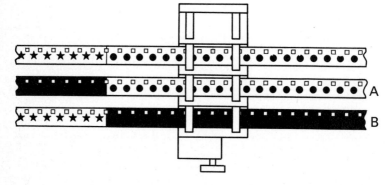

6 Wind all rolls on to the synchronizer, and check the alignment of all joins – A roll, B roll and cutting-copy.
7 Providing all is well, wind on to the next cut.

When assembling the reversal master, optical effects are very simply achieved.

A *fade-in* or *fade-out* is effected merely by fading the printer light in or out during printing. All that needs to be done when assembling the master is to mark on the edges of the end frame that a fade is required, and to note the footage in the printing instructions. The appropriate marks are scratched in the emulsion, care being taken to see that the scratches do not encroach on the picture area.

A *mix* (or *dissolve*) is in fact a fade-out exactly super-imposed on a fade-in. The cut on the cutting-copy is at the centre of the mix, so the master extends the appropriate number of frames either side of the cut. It is important, when working on the cutting-copy, to remember that where a forty-frame mix is desired twenty extra frames must be allowed for the overlap; i.e. the cut must be made at least twenty frames before the end of the shot, or there will not be enough master left on the end of the shot to assemble the mix.

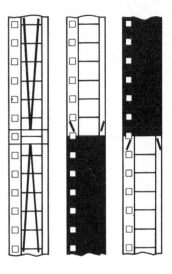

Marking fades in and out.

The procedure for assembling the mix is as follows. Note the frame number on the synchronizer at the cut on the cutting-copy. Then wind on twenty frames (this is for a forty-frame effect: opticals can vary from ten to ninety-six frames) and mark the master at this point. Now wind back forty frames from this point, and mark the black leader of the other roll.

Match up the edge number of the new master as usual, wind it back to this last mark, and mark the master. Wind out of the synchronizer, join at this mark, and wind back on to the mark on the outgoing master, which will be forty frames after the join just made. Cut the outgoing master at the mark, and splice on the black leader. Note the footage of the effect in the printing instructions: it is not essential to mark the fade-in and fade-out signs, although they may be included for absolute clarity.

Superimpositions are easy in A and B assembly: all that is necessary is to assemble the shot to be superimposed in the black leader at the appropriate place, and to note the footage in the printing instructions. The superimposed shot may be faded in or out as required, by marking up and noting in the usual way. Remember that superimposed titles on reversal stocks will always be white.

If the master film is negative rather than reversal, there are slight variations in assembly for optical effects.

For fades, a length of clear spacing must be incorporated in the non-picture roll for the exact forty frames of the fade. With reversal material, the gradual cutting out of the printer light produces a fade-out to black, since unexposed reversal stock processes black. With negative stock, how-ever, unexposed material processes clear, and a fading-out of the printer light would produce a white-out instead of a fade. The section of clear spacing incorporated in the other roll enables the print film to be fogged gradually as the image is faded, thus producing a fade-out to black. It will be noticed that a fade-out produced from negative has a slightly different appearance from one made from reversal master.

Otherwise, the negative assembly proceeds as with the reversal master. Continue working until all the master is assembled into A and B rolls, or until the rolls become too large (the labs will advise on maximum length of rolls for printing), when a fresh set should be started. After the last shot of the roll, leave 6 ft of black leader on both rolls before making a tail sync mark and punching it; follow with about 3 ft of white leader, with the obvious substitution of 'tail' for 'head' as the last notation. Then wind A roll, B roll and cutting-copy back slowly through the synchronizer, checking that all the splices are still in line, and that they are all good and sound.

However, mistakes do occur, and faulty alignment of cuts, if discovered on re-checking, must be rectified to prevent either a black frame printing through, or else an unintended superimposition of two frames. The point not to overlook in remedying such a mistake is that, if a frame is added or taken out in order to bring a splice into line, it will move all the succeeding splices out of sync for the rest of the reel. So any frame removed or added must be balanced out before the next splice: for every frame taken out, another must be put in, or vice versa. In some cases, the only remedy may be to remove one or two frames from both rolls. If this happens, the cutting-copy and all laid soundtracks must be adjusted so as to fit. If this is overlooked, the final sound-track will not fit the picture.

The best plan is to be meticulously careful at all stages of the master assembly; prevention of mistakes is straightforward, while rectification can be complex and time-consuming.

Note that picture-synchronizers are not usually suitable for A and B roll assembly, as they are more likely to scratch or damage the delicate master.

Packing and printing instructions

Once the master assembly is checked and correct, the film is ready for sending to the labs for printing. The film should be wound evenly and firmly on cores, head out, and packed carefully into cans. Any empty space in the cans should be padded out, to prevent the film sliding round, and all cans sealed with camera tape, and marked clearly on the outside with all relevant information about their contents.

The printing instructions should now be prepared: these will contain all information about the master, and about the print required, as itemized on pp. 107–8.

13 Sound editing

So far in this account we have mainly followed the progress of the picture from the rushes to the print. To discuss sound-track work after picture work is probably misleading; the division of the two is used here only for the sake of clarity. In fact, the laying of the sound-tracks – and all aspects of sound editing – must be considered as an integral part of film-editing, and must all be thought about at the same time. It is most important to realize that picture and sound are invariably cut together – the addition of a sound-track to a completed picture is, with the exception of a few limited kinds of film, an unrewarding and difficult task, and the results are almost bound to be less than satisfactory.

There are, inevitably, varying degrees of interaction between picture and sound. A 'Top of the Pops' record-illustration film, for example, starts with a completed sound-track and then adds a picture, whereas a news-reel takes available news picture, and adds a commentary and a suitably vague music track which can be rustled up in a trice, with a minimum of sound editing. But whatever the degree of interrelation between the picture and sound, the sound-track is a major creative contribution to the film, and must be constantly regarded as such – and not as merely a background to the pictures. The sound-track, moreover, is not nearly so evident to the audience as the picture: special camera effects and handsome camerawork will impress any audience, as will many forms of skilful picture cutting. Good sound recording and editing, even special effects sound work, will, on the other hand, be invariably taken for granted. This means two things: firstly the sound-track – recording and editing – must be technically well done, or the audience will become aware of it. Footsteps, for instance, that don't quite sound like footsteps, but like someone tapping their teeth, are a sure way of provoking the audience into laughter during a dramatic scene. Secondly, it means that the sound editor has considerable power to influence the audience's response to the film. Sounds can be very evocative indeed, and it is possible to have many layers of sound clearly comprehensible at one time. Kuleshov's famous 'montage' experiment* could surely, be repeated using sounds instead of associated images:

Picture – A man standing by a door. He does not move, his face shows no particular emotion.

* In this experiment, Kuleshov produced a series of sequences in each of which he intercut emotive images, connected with a specific feeling, with a facial close-up of an actor with as near neutral expression as possible. Each sequence was shown to a different audience, and, so it is said, each audience supposed the actor to be feeling the emotion suggested by the intercut images.

SOUND-TRACK	POSSIBLE RESPONSE
1 Sounds of revelry, singing, etc.	He's going to the party
2 Creaking floor, owl hoots, wind effects	The place is haunted
3 Shuffling and indeterminate clinking sounds	Mystery – who or what is there?
4 Electronic sounds	The Robotrons are after him
5 Heart-beats increasing in intensity	He's expecting someone to jump out and shoot him

And so on, *ad infinitum*. These possibilities only suggest effects: music, voices etc. will extend the range of response.

It is not only the nature of the sounds themselves that has an impact in the film, but the detailed positioning of those sounds. A fraction of a second's difference in the timing of an effect, for example, can drastically alter its impact. Take, for example, a shock cut from a quiet romantic scene to a CU of a motor-cycle roaring away from the camera. If the sound is brought in exactly with the picture, or fractionally before, the unexpected volume of the sound will give the audience a considerable jolt. If, on the other hand, the sound is not brought in until a second or so after the picture (or even less) the audience will have registered the image and so be expecting the sound. The effect will be greatly reduced.

Timing the commentary, too, is of similar importance. If the tie-up of the picture and the commentary is not accurate, the audience will be left for appreciable periods (which can be significant even when they last only half a second or so) wondering what a certain phrase refers to, or what an image is supposed to illustrate. Even slight lapses of this kind quickly build up to produce an unsettling effect in the audience's mind.

Accuracy, sensitivity and imagination are the chief qualities needed by the sound editor; and in all but large-scale pictures, the sound editor will probably be the picture editor too.

TRACK-LAYING PROCEDURE

Although some films will start picture cutting with the sound-track finally established – films involving precision cutting to music beats, for instance, or animated films, especially those with dialogue which requires a complete sound-track before shooting can even begin – track-laying will take place more or less concurrently with picture cutting. Most track-laying will be done in the late rough-cut and fine-cut stages, to enable modifications in the picture cutting to be made easily, while at the same time having a fairly good guide to the probable final shape of the picture.

The tracks laid are usually classified by the kind of sound they contain, into

sync tracks – shot with the picture
post-recorded dialogue etc.
commentary and voiceover tracks
effects (usually called FX) tracks
music tracks
loops – referring to the nature of the track rather than the
    sound it contains

The sync track (or tracks) will, of course, have been cut with the picture in all its stages, and is almost a self-laid track. The decisions to be made at this stage about the sync track are reduced virtually to questions of what level (sound-volume) to use, where to use the track, and where to omit it, and whether it can stand on its own, or needs reinforcement. All other tracks, however, must be recorded and laid by the sound editor, from scratch.

The first task is to collect and record all the sound necessary. Some sound may have been recorded on the location while shooting: sound effects difficult to obtain elsewhere, interviews for voiceover tracks, and perhaps some over-all guide-tapes to remind the editor of the total effect that he is trying to re-create. The editor will run through the rough cut of the picture, with the sync track if there is one, and note down where he has appropriate material to compile the track, and where more sound needs to be shot. At this stage he will be making broad policy decisions about the sound-track, and he will naturally be guided by the film's script. The script will not, though, contain details such as particular FX, for example, unless they make a specific point. The editor must fill all the gaps left in the script by careful examination of the cutting-copy.

The editor will now arrange for all outstanding sound to be recorded, including the commentary, which will probably involve the hiring of a professional commentator (which should have been allowed for in the budget, if required). Much of the music for the film may well be obtained from sound libraries: the relevant selection must be made and requested from the library, and copyright must be cleared.★ When all sound is collected together – probably mostly on $\frac{1}{4}$-in. magnetic tape – it is sent to the labs for transfer to 16-mm. magnetic film. If a certain amount of tape editing can be done before transfer, worthwhile savings can be made on transfer costs; in addition, large-scale editing of sound is usually easier on $\frac{1}{4}$-in. tape than it is on magnetic film. Large sections of unusable interview, for example, are easily excised, as are mistakes made during a

★ See p. 101.

commentary which have subsequently been re-recorded. Transcription of all interview and other voiceover material will make initial editing far easier: the time taken in writing all available speech down on paper will easily be made up in time saved during editing. It is much easier to turn over a page than to rewind 500 ft of tape, or change a spool of tape, to see if a phrase is repetitious, or to compare content.

The tapes for transfer should be sent to the labs with all details of the recordings, and of the transfer required. Check that edge-track (E/T) or centre-track (C/T) is chosen according to the editing equipment to be used, and also that it is consistent for all sound throughout the film.

Once the sound is all transferred to 16-mm. film, the building up of the tracks on to the film can begin in a synchronizer. Each sound-track should have a white leader containing all information, followed by 6 ft of black leader with a sync mark level with that on the cutting-copy, e.g.

Marking up sound track leaders.

Care must be taken that all tracks and all stages of picture are kept in correct synchronization – lost sync can be troublesome to trace and rectify.

The sound takes on magnetic film can now be separated and hung up on clip racks like action takes – although some takes may well be too long to hang up conveniently like this. Music and commentary, for example, may continue unbroken through many cuts in the picture, and these takes on magnetic film can be rolled up, on or off their cores, and stored in clearly labelled cans. All sound takes must have their content and direction of travel marked on them as soon as the sound rushes are cut up. Failure to label sound takes can cause much time to be wasted in running bits of magnetic film over playback heads for identification.

Tracks can be built up one at a time, or up to as many as three at a time on a four-way synchronizer. In the early stages it is as well to make a rough assembly of each track separately to the picture. Then, when all the tracks have been put together, they can be checked against each other, and minor adjustments made to the tracks and the picture as necessary. At this stage of the proceedings, work is made much easier by the use of a picture-synchronizer (pic-sync), which incorporates a viewing screen into the first channel; this enables the sound and picture to be run through to-gether locked in level sync, so that the sound for each frame is directly in line with it on the synchronizer. In more advanced stages of track-laying, of course, editing-machines are essential, both for the picture, as described above, and for running the sound to the correct speed, to judge its effect. Music, particularly, is very difficult to hear clearly

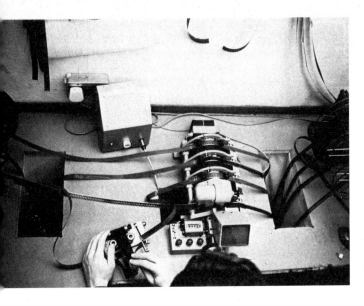

Track-laying with pic-sync and
CIR tape splicer.

on hand-wound synchronizers, especially if it contains no
marked beats. The more sophisticated editing-tables are also
invaluable in later stages of track-laying, in order to run
two or three tracks together with the picture, and thus to
judge how the various tracks will interact with each other,
and how the total effect will fit to the picture. If the editing-
table has mixing facilities, the editor can make a series
of trial mixes: the best one can then be sent to the dubbing
studio to guide the dubbing mixer when the final mix is
made.

Whatever equipment is used, the laying of the tracks
continues until the full sound-track is composed. It is usual
to block in spaces between sound takes with discarded
exposed filmstock, although specially coated leader is
preferable. However, care should be taken to ensure that
there is at least one track incorporating magnetic film –
modulated or unmodulated – at all points of the film. If there
is a continuous sync track, there will be no problem, but if,
for example, FX only are to be used in a film, care must be
taken that all spaces are filled by magnetic film on at least one
track, otherwise, if any gaps appear, the 'drop-out' of the
background noise will be noticeable. 'Fill' or 'shush' (see p.
102) can be used to level out drop-outs.

Each roll of sound-track should be completed with tail
leaders and tail sync marks, as for the ends of all rolls of
material. When they are completed, they should be rewound firmly and evenly, put in cans, and the cans clearly
labelled. Splices should be re-checked during re-winding:
splices on magnetic film, it should be remembered, are
always made with the tape splicer on the cell side only, and
using the diagonal cut.

In addition to these laid tracks, matched on the synchronizer with the picture, there may well be other sound

material to be arranged for the final dubbing sessions. First, disks may be used in the mix: most labs will offer at least one disk play-off, and this may be the most convenient source from which to swing in some sections of general background effect or music. Second, $\frac{1}{4}$-in. tape play-offs may also be incorporated in the same way; if some general sound can be mixed direct from tape, some transfer cost and track-laying time may be saved. And thirdly, probably the most widely used form of non-laid track is the loop – a section of magnetic film joined end to end in a continuous loop which can be threaded up into a replay channel in the mixing equipment, and brought in and out when required. Obviously, this system has only limited uses: mainly for atmosphere tracks, and for very general effects, and sound intended for use in loops must obviously not contain any marked feature which will become noticeable on repetition. Common examples of the use of loops are background traffic effect, external country atmosphere, babbling brooks, and so forth. If loops are to be used, the maximum length acceptable to the dubbing studio should be ascertained, and the loop made up and sent in a marked can. Mark, on the loop itself, its content and its direction of travel. When making the join in the loop, be careful to choose a cutting point where the flow of sound will be uninterrupted: a change of level, or a sound cut halfway, reappearing every ten seconds soon becomes noticeable.

THE DUBBING CHART

When all the tracks are complete, and all final adjustments have been made to picture and sound, the dubbing chart (or cue sheet) must be compiled, to inform the dubbing mixer of the contents of the sound-tracks, and the editor's intentions as to their mixing. Again, accuracy is imperative in the compilation of the dubbing chart. The dubbing mixer at the sound studio will be completely fresh to the film, and the dubbing chart is the communication link through which the editor tells the mixer about the film. If possible, the editor should arrange to be present at the dubbing session of his film: if he cannot attend, full detailed instructions about anything unusual should be written in addition to the dubbing chart.

Some labs will issue their own blanks for dubbing charts; where this is the case, these should always be used, as their mixers will be used to working from them. Where no particular pattern is issued, a general-purpose cue sheet can be obtained from editor's suppliers, or a piece of blank paper ruled into columns will do. For small-gauge film-making, vertical columns are normally used: some features companies use horizontal charts for some tracks. One column is used to represent each track, and each column is headed by its description and number. Sections of the column are blocked in to represent sections of sound in that track; footage numbers at the beginning and end of the section are written in, and blocks are sometimes coloured, for easier recognition. The nature of the sound is written in the block; in the left-hand column, the action cues – footages and brief descriptions of the pictures – are noted.

Fade-outs and fade-ins on the sound are indicated by pointed (instead of straight) ends to the block; where a fade-in on one track coincides with a fade-out on another, a sound mix is shown. Where one track fading under another is desired, the block is narrowed from either side in the track to fade down; the superimposed track remains at full column width.

Loops, disks and tapes each have a column to themselves; there may well be more than one of each used, and in this case a fresh column should be drawn up. Many loops and disks may be available from the library at the dubbing studio, especially widely used effects and atmospheres. It is worth checking with the studio to see if they can supply the sound required; as a general rule, however, it is safer to hear the sound before it is incorporated into a sound-track, and if the editor cannot be present for the dubbing session, it will be wiser if he prepares all his own sound where possible.

A dubbing chart may well become very involved, with many tracks, but, for example, a simple track may look like this:

ACTION	MUSIC	DIAL.	FX1	FX2	LOOP	Remarks
000						
L.S. Western desert: horse appears on horizon: comes toward camera			025 Hooves L.S.		Western exterior atmosphere	
054	054					Please supply loop from library.
M.C.U. Horse stops. Man looks down.			054	054 C.U. Hooves horse stops.		
086						
Old hobo						Keep atmos. low.
091		091 Hero: "Which way to Laramie?"	091 Hooves; Bridle jingling.	091		
C.U. Hero						
100				103 Hobo spits 104		
Hobo spits: points.		109 Hero: "Yipee!"				
109						
C.U. Hero				111 Horse galloping away.		
111		"Hi/yoo!"				
He gallops off						
134	134					Music swells behind title.
Main title.						

Typical dubbing chart.

Colouring the blocks with a different colour for each track may assist legibility; in any case pay maximum attention to neatness and clarity, as the dubbing mixer will have to read the chart while at the same time looking at the picture projected on a screen, and at a footage counter, with his hands working the volume control slides. Any difficulty with reading the dubbing chart can only make his job more difficult, and a satisfactory result less likely.

When the dubbing chart is completed, it is packed off with the various tracks to the dubbing studio for the final mix. Once the mixed magnetic master has returned from the studio, it should be carefully checked against the cutting-copy of the picture, and the general quality of the sound checked. If it is satisfactory, it can now be sent with the picture master to the labs for the final printing on to the married print, either as an optical track printed on photographically, or by a further magnetic transfer to a magnetic stripe applied by the labs.

A good exercise in understanding sound editing is to put a reel of a feature film on a Moviola, and analyse the sound-track by attempting to reconstruct the dubbing chart.

THE ANSWER PRINT AND RELEASE PRINTS

When the labs have received all the master material – sound and picture – they will examine the master and produce a report on its state, and will grade the master for printing. The grading of the master will be carried out by an experienced grader; basically, this involves assessing the master to judge what variations in printer light are going to be needed to produce an evenly exposed and visually consistent print. Since even the most experienced cameramen are liable to get slightly varying exposures over the shooting of an entire film – and lesser cameramen may get wide discrepancies – a large degree of control in the printing exposure of the final print may be required. Because a film presents a continuous succession of images, it is very important that the texture of those images remains constant except, obviously, when there is good reason for variation. The grader will assess the printing requirements of the master, and will mark the master to trigger off automatic adjustments in the printer. These triggering marks will differ according to the kind of printer being used: they might, for instance, be small cuts made in the side of the film, or pieces of aluminium foil affixed to the edge. On most modern printers, however, the operation is controlled by punched tape.

If the film is to be printed in colour, the grader will also assess any colour correction needed. Since variations in exposure on colour stock produce variation in colour rendering as well as in image density, this must also be evened out in the printing. A colour analyser is used by the grader to help him to make his decisions, and the master film is marked to trigger off the necessary adjustments to the printer.

When the master has been graded or colour-corrected, and the mixed magnetic sound master has been transferred to an optical negative, the first print of the film is made. This is the approval print, more usually known as the answer print: in many cases of small-unit films this may be the only copy to be made, but for films where more copies are required, the approval print is returned to the film-maker before further prints are taken. The director and editor of the film, and perhaps the film's sponsor, will look at the film, and may make last-minute adjustments to details of grading and colour matching, and will look out for any faults that may have crept in. They will also want to see that the general quality of the printing is up to the expected standard. If everything is not satisfactory, the film-maker may want to order another approval print; but providing all is now well, the order for the release prints – the prints that will be used for exhibition – will now be placed with the labs. When these are returned and checked, the film-maker's job is finished.

Before the release prints are ordered, however, there remain one or two practical decisions to be made. The master of any film can only be good for a certain number of prints. If, say, thirty prints or more are likely to be needed of a film, it will be as well to order a duplicate (dupe) master to be made before any prints are taken from the original master. The release prints can then be taken from the dupe master, which can be replaced when badly worn by a further dupe from the original master. Dupe masters can be made in reversal or negative (when they are known as 'internegatives') form, or even reduced to a smaller gauge: the editor must decide which format he needs.

Secondly, mixed magnetic masters, like all magnetic recordings, run the risk of accidental erasure or deterioration. If further prints of the film are likely to be needed at some future date, it is advisable to cut risks, and have duplicates made of all master material.

Finally, most labs will store all kinds of master material under suitable storage conditions for fairly modest charges. After all the work that has gone into the preparation of the film, it is probably worth while to safeguard the results.

14 Presentation

The final approved print returns from the printing labs; the last stage in the cycle of film-making is projection and presentation, which, as with all aspects of the making of the film, should be carried out with care and accuracy. Projection is the final link in the chain of communication between the film-maker and his audience, and shortcomings in this area are as distracting to an audience as are faults in camera-work or editing. Occasional breaks in the film are perhaps inevitable, but a thorough understanding of projection machinery and technique will ensure that even these are kept to a minimum, and that the film will be shown in the most satisfactory way possible.

THE PROJECTOR

The movie projector is essentially a camera in reverse, with light passing through the film from inside the projector to the outside, instead of from outside the camera to the inside. As with the camera, a lens is used to focus the image sharply on the receiving plane – in this case the screen – and an intermittent movement combined with a shutter is used in a similar way to the camera, to bring a rapid sequence of still images into position in the gate, where light passes through the film and projects the image on to the screen.

The essential features of the projector are a feed and take-up system; a main drive system operating the sprockets; the intermittent movement and the shutter; stabilizing rollers; the film gate and pressure plate; a light source and cooling system; and a sound-reproduction system.

The feed and take-up are effected by spools mounted on arms and usually accommodate reels of film up to 1,600 or 2,000 ft in capacity, giving running times of up to approximately forty-five minutes on one reel. Care must be taken when loading that spools are put on correctly, and secured in position: feed spools, in particular, are liable to fall off during projection if not secured, and a film break is then almost certain, as well as the scratching of many feet of film. Further, check that spools are not bent or distorted: a bent take-up spool will spill projected film on to the floor and damage may result.

The main drive system is an electric motor, often with adjustable running speed, which drives all moving parts of the projector. The sprocket wheels give the main power to the film transport, pushing and pulling the film to and from the gate area with a continuous movement; the shutter rotates on its spindle and cuts off light between the source and the film gate during the image change-over; the intermittent claw mechanism at the gate of the projector, like the intermittent movement of the camera, keeps each frame stationary in front of the gate for a fraction of a second while the shutter is open. The feed and take-up systems, the rewind facility and the lamp cooling fan also run from the main motor. There are no routine adjustments to be made to the drive mechanism, except to clean all exposed parts regularly and thoroughly, and to regulate the motor to the correct running speed. With some models the running speed may be controlled only by a two-way switch: on projectors with infinitely variable speed settings, such as the Siemens 2000, the running speed should be checked frequently – in this case by the strobe disk.

The aperture in the film gate, and its corresponding pressure-plate aperture, frame the light, so that the area of light passing through the film is the same as the frame size on the film. Fine adjustments to the exact positioning of the gate aperture are effected by the framing (or 'racking') adjusting knob. Ensure that the gate area is kept clean; any dirt in the gate aperture will project on to the screen, while dirt in the film channel can soon become compacted hard enough to scratch film during projection.

A range of lenses is available for film projectors, though they differ from camera lenses in that they do not have variable apertures. The most commonly used focal length for projection lenses on 16-mm. projectors is 2 in. The shorter the focal length of the lens, the larger the projected image over a given throw, but the larger the image, the more the light must spread, and the less intense it will become. For projection over throws of between 20 and 40 ft – which covers most average projection areas for 16-mm. – the 2-in. (50 mm.) lens is usually found to give the best compromise between image size and brightness. For reference, the difference in picture width between a 1-in. and a 2-in. projection lens at given distances is as follows:

	10 ft	15 ft	20 ft	25 ft	30 ft	35 ft	40 ft
1-in. (25 mm.)	3′ 11″	5′ 10″	7′ 9″	9′ 8″	11′ 8″	13′ 7″	—
2-in. (50 mm.)	1′ 11″	2′ 10″	3′ 10″	4′ 9″	5′ 9″	6′ 8″	7′ 8″

At 40 ft, with a 1-in. lens, the light intensity from most projectors will have fallen off to such an extent that the picture will be unsatisfactory.

Lenses of many different focal lengths may be obtained to provide pictures of greater, smaller or intermediate sizes. Anamorphic (or 'scope') lenses, which produce wide-screen images from 'squeezed' prints, are also obtainable for 16-mm. projectors, either as a complete lens which replaces the normal projection lens in its housing, or as an attachment which fits in front of the normal projection lens. It is worth remembering, since anamorphic lenses are fairly expensive to buy and may not be used very often, that most film-hire firms will also hire out 16-mm. scope lenses or attachments together with scope prints. All details of projector – make, gauge and model – must be given when hiring lenses, since there is no standard fitment, and different support brackets are necessary for different projectors.

Several types of light source are used in 16-mm. projectors, and new developments have recently taken place in this field. The tungsten projector lamps which have been standard until the last year or two are gradually being replaced with quartz-iodine and tungsten-halogen bulbs, which give greater light output from a smaller unit, and which are very much cooler than previous lamps. This means that smaller cooling-fans can be used, and projector noise is considerably reduced. The new light sources are also longer-lasting than previous types, and the incidence of bulb failure during projection is now much smaller. However, it will be several years yet before all of the older type of light sources pass out of service, and, since there are differing types of lamps, it is important to be certain which type is fitted to the projector to be used, as some types of lamp require special treatment. The very high-powered 'marc' lamps, for instance, which can give enough light output to enable 16-mm. projectors and film to be used for full-scale theatrical presentation, require warming-up and cooling-off periods in order to give best results and maximum life. Since these lamps can cost £15 and upwards, it is worth ascertaining any special conditions of operation.

In all cases, check that the correct bulb is being used in each projector. Most projectors run either at mains voltage (240 V) or at 110 V through a transformer, and lamps of various wattage are obtainable in each voltage. Check that the lamp chosen does not draw more than the maximum recommended amperage (remembering that watts/volts= amps) for the projector, or overheating of the lamp base or the lampholder may cause projector failure. Some projectors have external transformers to convert the mains supply to the required voltage, and in some cases these are adjustable. These too must be set to the correct output. Remember, in any cases of doubt or incompatibility, that it is safer to 'underrun' a lamp (i.e. supply it with a lower voltage than that marked on it), which will give lower light output, but lengthen its life, than to overrun it (supply a higher voltage than marked), when the light output would be greater, but the life of the lamp would be unpredictable; with severe overrunning the bulb would blow at once.

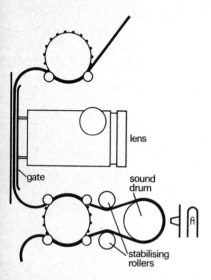

Typical projector threading path.

lens

gate

sound drum

stabilising rollers

PROJECTION PROCEDURE

First of all, and before every reel of film is projected, clean the projector thoroughly. Clean all exposed moving parts, and everywhere the film touches during projection. Particular attention must be paid to the film gate area – the lens carriage will either swing open or be easily removable for access. All specks of emulsion, which always collect during projection, should be brushed clear; if any deposit is caked on hard, it should be pushed off gently with a matchstick or something similar – never with a metal tool, as the slightest damage to the material of the film path may result in continuous scoring of the film during projection. Lenses can be cleaned gently with a soft brush, and, if necessary, a selvyt cloth; clean both ends of the projection lens, as both are exposed to dust. The sound heads, too, are points for particular attention when cleaning, and every so often all rollers, sprocket wheels and film-retaining devices must be checked.

When the projector has been cleaned, it should be switched on to allow the amplifier (and the lamp, if necessary) to warm up. The film is then laced into the threading path. There will probably be a diagram indicating the threading path either on the casing of the projector itself, or in the handbook, and it is most important that the threading path be followed accurately. Faulty lacing-up of the projector is a common cause of breakdown during projection, and of consequent film damage.

Although the layout of different types of projector may differ slightly in detail, all threading paths will incorporate the same features. The film is clipped on to two drive wheels with sprockets, one before and one after the gate area, which provide the main transport of the film; the positioning of the retaining clips should be checked, as incorrect positioning of the sprockets may result in torn film. Between the drive sprocket wheels and the gate will be a loop, as in the camera, to absorb the intermittent movement of the claw mechanism at the gate; as with the camera, if the loops are too small the film may snap, while if they are too large, the film may wear through contact with the projector casing. In addition, the sound heads of the projector are at an exact distance from the picture gate, and the sound relating to each picture is an exact number of frames ahead. Thus, if the bottom loop on the projector is either too large or too small, too few or too many frames will separate the picture from the sound, resulting in loss of synchronization. The lens carriage will either hinge outwards or slide forwards to allow the introduction of the film into the gate area. It is best to operate the projector's inching knob until the claw is in the withdrawn position while inserting the film; the inching knob can then be used to ascertain that the claws have engaged, before running the projector.

The sound heads are positioned by the sound drum, which is attached to a flywheel to ensure smooth running. The film passes through a stabilizing roller device to smooth out any intermittent movement remaining after the bottom loop, before arriving at the sound drum. When lacing up, it is most important to ensure that the film fits snugly round the sound drum. Any slackness here will result in poor sound reproduction of both magnetic and optical tracks. From the sound drum the film passes through the second drive sprocket, under a few guide-rollers, and on to the take-up spool.

An increasing number of projectors now incorporate an automatic threading system, whereby the film is fed into the first drive sprocket wheel, and is then carried through the threading path by the projector drive system, and only requires attaching to the take-up spool when it emerges. The essential features of automatic threading machines are two loop-formers, one either side of the gate, which guide the film in an appropriate path, so as to create the correct-sized loop. The loop-formers must be set in position before feeding film into the machine; after threading they must be returned to their normal position. Each automatic-threading projector will have detailed operating instructions supplied.

When the film is laced up, the projector motor should run for a moment or two in order to check that the threading is correct, and then be switched on to run off the leader of the reel: the projector's running speed may also be corrected, if necessary, during this time. In addition to its protective layers of coated and/or black leader, the film will have one of two standard numbered leaders – an Academy leader, or an SMPTE (Society of Motion Picture and Television Engineers) leader. A third type of leader (the BBC) is used internally by BBC television, and may be encountered occasionally. The leaders give a countdown to the first picture frame, numbered, at one-second intervals at 24 f.p.s, from 11 down to 3. The projected numbers of the leaders may be sufficient for the projectionist to focus and frame the image on the screen: if not, the first few feet of picture can be used, and at any rate this alignment and adjustment of the projector should be carried out well before the showing time. The focusing knob, to be found on the lens carriage, will move the lens bodily towards or from the film plane. The frame-line adjuster, which alters the positioning of the gate aperture, is usually placed above or beside the gate itself. Great care should be given to focusing and framing: both fuzzy focus and visible frame lines can be of real annoyance to an audience, and can prevent their involvement with, or mar their enjoyment of, the film. The alignment of the projector and screen must be made so that the image appears as rectangular as possible (angling of the projector in relation to the screen will produce slightly wedge-shaped images), and the sound volume should be set to the most acceptable level. When these checks have been carried out, the film can be returned to the beginning of the reel, and is now ready for projection to an audience.

The projectionist should stay by the projector as long as the film is running; adjustments to the framing and focusing may occasionally have to be made, and when the reel is finished, the light source should be switched off in order to avoid projecting the tail leader. If there is another reel of the same film to follow, the timing of the change-over will be indicated by two marks on the projected image – usually circles in the top right-hand corner of the frame, about seven seconds apart. The first indicates that the second projector should be switched on – the leader of the second reel of the film will have been placed in the gate at the correct position, determined by experiment with the particular projector – and by the time the second change-over mark appears, the leader in the second projector will have been run off, the projector will be running to speed, and the change-over will be made either by an automatic coupling switch, or by hand operation of the two switches.

Mishaps do occur during projection, even during the best-prepared shows; but they can mostly be anticipated, and the disruption they cause kept to a minimum. Bulbs and fuses do blow: always have spares to hand, and make sure that the location and the method of fitting of all fuses and lamps – including the sound exciter lamp – is known. If electrical connections, leads, plugs and sockets are checked periodically they should not give trouble during shows. Film, however, does occasionally tear during projection. Stop the projector at once, and repair the film; a good-quality hot splicer is best, and if a temporary repair has to be made with an unsuitable splicer, a note should be made to repair the break properly later; or if the film is hired, the library should be informed.

Loss of loop below the projector gate is another frequent mishap during projection, and is usually caused by torn perforations in the film. When the bottom loop is lost, the claw can no longer function, and a blurred and unregistered image appears on the screen. Again, stop the projector immediately, and reform the loop; withdraw the claw by operating the inching knob until the film in the gate slides freely, and pull through enough film to make the loop up to the right size again. The top loop will then need reforming by repositioning the sprocket holes on the top drive wheel. The whole operation of reforming the loop should only take a few seconds: some projectors are even equipped with an automatic loop-restoring device that will cut out most trouble from this source.

Sudden loss of sound quality is usually attributable to the film path over the sound heads, if the sound-track is known to be in good condition. Loose threading round the sound drum is easily overlooked, and can cause bad fluttering in the sound reproduction; on magnetic tracks, loss of volume and poor general quality may well be the result of accumulated dust and emulsion on the magnetic head. The other usual cause of sound loss is the failure of the exciter lamp, although these only burn out comparatively rarely. All these sound faults are quickly remedied, but obviously require the projector to be stopped; it is better to do this immediately the fault is detected, rather than hoping it will go away if it

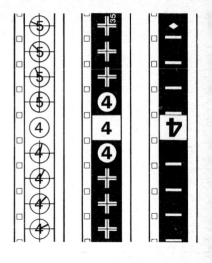

Standard projection leaders.

is left for another 100 ft. Hearing difficulties, or distracting interferences with the sound, are damaging to the audience's response to the film.

Finally, a word about 'green prints'. When a print has just been made and processed, it retains a little moisture, and is in the condition known as 'green'. This will only last for a short time, but may result in picture unsteadiness, and handling problems such as uneven take-up winding. There is not much that can be done if this happens, but it may be the explanation for otherwise puzzling symptoms.

PROJECTION CONDITIONS

The conditions in the room to be used for projection will have considerable effect on the quality of the presentation. First, the blackout must be good, and checked for annoying minor light leaks. Secondly, the seating should be arranged so that all seats are within the optimum viewing area for the type of screen in use. The height of the screen above the audience must be decided, as well as the positioning of the speakers. A single speaker is often placed centrally below the screen, but may be better sited to the side of the screen, two-thirds of the way up. Placing the speaker behind the screen, even if there is room, is unnecessary, and can muffle or distort the sound. Twin speakers can be positioned at either end of the screen, or in the corners of the room at the screen end. Experiment will show the way in which the available speakers can best be suited to the acoustics of the room: remember that at least some of the experimenting should be done with the room full of people, since the audience considerably affects the acoustics of an auditorium.

There is some choice in the type of material used for screens. Beaded screens, with the surface covered by small glass beads, give a very high light reflectance and a bright picture, but the image brightness falls off very sharply when viewed from an angle: this type of screen is most suitable for long narrow auditoria where most of the audience is seated directly in front of the screen. A matt white screen gives a picture that is equally bright over a much wider angle of viewing, although it is never equal to that of a beaded screen viewed from directly in front. Silvered matt screens give a little more picture brightness than matt white; both are suitable for squarish rooms. Translucent screens are frequently used for back-projection purposes, and often incorporate a quasi-prismatic surface on one side to increase brightness. Such screens are often used for viewing under daylight conditions.

Whatever type of screen material is used, presentation will be improved if the picture area is masked off with a matt black material. This will rectify any slight misalignment of projector and screen, avoiding the slightly wedge-shaped pictures that sometimes occur, and will also hide any slight variation in image area between two projectors at change-over. The black masking will also cut out the ill-defined edge of the picture that is inevitable with 16-mm. over a long throw, and give clean edges to the image.

SOUND REPRODUCTION

The sound-track of the film is recorded either on a band of magnetic recording material (magnetic stripe) which is laid along the non-perforated side of the film, and which operates like the tape in a tape recorder, or else by an area of the film which to varying degrees interrupts a narrow beam of light (from the exciter lamp) thrown on to a photo-electric cell: the varying electrical impulses thus produced are translated via an amplifier and speaker into the sound as recorded. This is known as an optical sound-track, and the variation in light-interruption can be produced either by a band of uniform width but varying density, or by a band of uniform density but variable width. These are known as variable-density and variable-area tracks respectively: the variable-area is now favoured. Both types of sound-track are prepared the same way in the editing-room; the mixed magnetic master may then either be recorded direct on to a magnetic stripe applied to the print, or can be transferred to an optical negative (or reversal master) track, which is printed and processed along with the visuals of the film.

The reproduction facilities for optical sound-tracks are standard on all 16-mm. sound projectors, and most commercially hired films will have an optical track. The quality of sound recording, however, is generally inferior to that of magnetic stripe recordings, but has the great advantage of universality, since many 16-mm. projectors are not equipped to replay magnetic sound. Optical tracks are also proof against accidental erasure: since most projectors capable of magnetic play-back can also record and erase, careless operation may lead to total or partial erasure of the existing sound-track. For these reasons, if films are intended for wide use they should be provided with an optical track. Where there are to be large numbers of prints, too, optical tracks may prove to be cheaper than magnetic ones; once the optical master is prepared – although this is a relatively expensive procedure for a film of which only one or two copies are required – it can be printed many times over, the only further cost being the charge for an additional roll in printing. The cost of magnetic striping and dubbing to striped prints will begin to add up if more than a few copies are made.

For single copies, though, magnetic sound is considerably cheaper, and for certain types of very limited sound-track it is possible to use direct recording via a suitable projector, and thus save all the costs of transfer, track-laying, mixing and the final dubbing. Generally, only simple tracks such as a single voice, or voice and music, can be done in this way, but pre-mixed tapes, for tracks where there is no spot synchronization, can provide more elaborate compilations.

In the movie projector, the sound heads are at a fixed distance from the gate aperture: the optical head is nearer, at twenty-six frames past the gate, and the magnetic head comes two frames later, at twenty-eight frames past the gate. These distances are standard, and are allowed for by the labs when the sound is put on to the film: maintaining the correct size of the bottom loop when threading the projector will ensure that synchronization of sound and picture is kept. Since even one or two frames of error in sync are noticeable on the screen, it is very important to ensure accuracy at this point. Cleanliness and maintenance of the sound heads, as mentioned above, are vital to ensure that the soundtrack is reproduced with its full quality.

During the editing of the film, it will frequently be necessary to project the cutting-copy together with the soundtrack on a separate magnetic film, in order to judge the progress of the editing. It will also be necessary to project the final cutting-copy together with the final mix of the sound, before ordering the final print. On these occasions, and at any other time when the picture and sepmag. sound must be projected, a 'double-band' or 'double-head' projector is necessary. This will probably be a standard projector, with an attachment (on the opposite side to the picture-film transport mechanism) allowing magnetic sound film to be run and replayed in sync at the same time as the picture is run through the normal side of the projector. As with the picture projector, each double-band attachment will have its own design and threading path, but basically, they will all comprise a magnetic sound replay head, a stabilizing flywheel, and a drive sprocket linked mechanically to the picture drive. Normally the picture film will be laced with its sync mark in the gate and the sound film with its sync mark by the sound head; though in some models, the sound sync mark may be placed a couple of frames ahead of the replay head to allow for take-up in the stabilizing rollers. Both sides of the projector will be controlled from a single switch, and viewing the film will be similar to viewing a married print.

CARE OF THE PRINT

The print has only a limited life: in due course it will become so scratched and damaged that it will no longer be fit to show. But thoughtful care of the print, so long and expensive in preparation, will ward off that time for as long as possible.

The most important single factor in the well-being of the print is to ensure that it is treated with care in normal use. Make sure that it is projected carefully, through clean projectors, and that it is rewound carefully after projection. If possible, it is kinder to rewind the film by hand: rewind reasonably slowly, and keep a moderate tension so as to get a firmly wound film. Loosely wound film will scratch itself: but never try to pull a loosely wound print tight –

Siemens double-band projector;
(*left*) 16-mm. magnetic sound side
of this projector.

this 'skinching' will do more damage still. Also, do not try
to tap down bits of film that have not wound level. Leave
them, or rewind again. Ensure that films are well protected
by good leaders at both ends, and always keep film on spools
that are in good condition – smooth, and not bent. The plastic spools which are becoming ever more popular are kind
to films, but should be discarded if they become warped.

While rewinding, inspect prints for scratches. If any serious
damage is noticed, check the equipment immediately, to
avoid subsequent damage to other films. Bad scratching on
the print can be remedied fairly successfully by a 'scratch
treatment' at the labs: even deep scoring can be quite well
covered up. For routine wear and dust, an occasional clean
with a soft cloth impregnated with film cleaner will be
helpful. But a good way of protecting the print as soon as it
is processed is to have it waxed by the labs. This will give the
film a long-lasting protective coating, and help to reduce
friction during projection.

Finally, a note about storage and transport. Films must be
stored in a cool, even temperature, in as clean an atmosphere
as possible. If the film is to be stored for any length of time,
take care that it is wound firmly and evenly on its spool, and
that it is kept in a can. For transporting, the film, wound
firmly on a projection spool, placed in its can, and clearly
labelled with all relevant details, should be packed in a fibre
box and, if necessary, padded. If film has to be packed while
wound on a core, make sure that it is well padded in its can,
to prevent rattling and sliding. And when posting films, do
not forget to register the parcel, or at least to send it by
recorded delivery. When returning a film to a film library,
a certificate of posting should be obtained: the films will
then generally be covered by the renter's insurance.

Master material, after printing, should be wound and
stored even more carefully than the print, since further

prints may be needed of the same film. If more prints are likely to be required within a short time, it may be as well to ask the labs to store the master.

THE MARKET

Once the film is complete and ready for projection, the question of where to show it arises. Unless it is a sponsored film, or a film made privately for some particular organization or body – a charity, for example – there may be no obvious market outside the film-maker's circle of friends; and a film needs to be shown. Moreover, a film needs an organized audience: the very business of projection means that the film is not a medium which, like most others, can be enjoyed by a succession of single viewers, readers or listeners.

Markets for non-professional films are not yet organized with any conviction, although this may well be remedied in the next few years. There are, however, a number of outlets to look out for: these are continually increasing, and the following suggestions are only a beginning.

First, there are a number of non-professional and student film festivals, although the number and location of these does tend to vary from year to year. One well-established festival is Southampton University's 'Motion' festival, which for several years now has been attracting a wide range of non-professional films, and presenting them in a serious and organized way. In London, the London School of Film and the Royal College of Art Department of Film and TV have both staged festivals in recent years, though neither has yet established a recognized national event.

Internationally, there are many competitions and festivals which are open to non-professionally made films; some are regular events, while others are once-off events, revolving round one subject or theme. An 'Icograda' competition, for example, in 1968, took human rights as its theme, while another more recent event in Canada concentrated on films about climbing and mountaineering. These events must be sought out carefully, as many of them are not very widely publicized. The National Panel for Film Festivals, however, has details of most of the regular major festivals, and can often help with information about smaller ones. The Glasgow Amateur Festival, which is run by the Scottish Film Council, and attracts international attention, is one of the very best of the many amateur film festivals, and has a reputation for liveliness and quality.

The British National Film Catalogue publishes particulars of all new films released in Britain, and appears quarterly. Details of all films intended for release should be sent to this publication. It is the standard reference work of its kind, and films entered in it will attract a certain amount of attention.

The Film Library of the British Film Institute carries a selection of non-professional films, and is constantly viewing material which may be suitable for their distribution system.

However, the number of films of this kind that they can handle is fairly limited, and probably only very good films will be accepted here. Outstanding non-professional films, or films containing very unusual material, may also very occasionally get a showing on TV. Both the BBC and commercial TV occasionally show such films.

There is a growing 'underground' market for 16-mm. and even 8-mm. non-professional movies; this is an excellent outlet for films, and often reaches audiences sympathetic to the kind of film that it is hard to show elsewhere. Organizations such as the London Film-Makers Co-operative run extensive catalogues of films, and charge a very small commission on bookings made through them. Other co-operatives are active in other areas of the country (although their functioning is not always consistent), and the Arts Lab movement also provides a worthwhile market for personal films.

Finally, there are a number of organizations that are interested in promoting non-professional film-making, and film education. The British Film Institute is useful in some ways, especially its Education Department, as is the Experimental Film Board, which, under certain circumstances, can supply financial backing for non-professional films. Details of conditions and services can be obtained from the BFI. The British Kinematographic Society (BKS) has an Education Committee which, while chiefly concerned with promoting film education in its more formal aspects, can also often help with many kinds of advice. The Film Education Network is also interested in the same kind of activity, and together with the film-publishing firm Attic is working towards coordinating information on non-professional film-making, and also towards organizing markets. The Arts Council of Great Britain, and the regional Arts Associations, are increasingly interested in films, and already subsidize and distribute many film projects, as well as organizing competitions and awards.

These, it should be emphasized, are only a few of the places that may be of use to the film-maker when he has finished his film. He will have to work to a certain extent to create his own market: there is always somewhere that will show films. Local schools, charities and societies may be glad to have films available for showing at little or no cost; colleges and universities may compile programmes of locally made films. At all events, a film is made for an audience; once the time and money have been spent on making a film, it is a pity to leave it rolled up in a can for ever. And from the film-maker's point of view, to see his own film in front of a completely neutral audience will be one of the most nerve-racking and instructive stages in the whole process of making the film. All the minor imperfections that he had learned to pass over during the making of the film now stand out like sore thumbs: probably more to the film-maker himself than to the audience. It is a salutary experience. This is the final test: this is what it has all been for.

Glossary

ACTION
The picture film – a term particularly used during the editing of the film, when the action and sound are separate.

ACTION
The director's command to the actor(s) or subject(s) to start.

ANSWER PRINT
The initial print produced by the labs from the graded negative/master. It is then vetted by the director, editor, sponsor etc., and any necessary alterations made to the grading before release prints are ordered. Two or more answer prints may be required in some instances.

ATMOS
'Atmosphere' – a background and often barely noticeable sound effect, e.g. 'country atmos', 'underground atmos'.

BABY-LEGS
A very short tripod.

BARNDOORS
Adjustable metal flaps (two or four) fixed to the front of photographic lamp heads, enabling the light beam to be cut off to desired extents.

BLIMP
A sound-deadening camera casing, to prevent camera motor noise reaching the microphone during sync shooting.

BLUES
Blue filters, either glass or gel, affixed to photographic lamps to raise the colour temperature to that of daylight, thus enabling mixed artificial and daylight to be used with colour film-stocks.

BUZZ (also 'fill' and 'shush')
Almost undetectable sound recorded and transferred to 16 mm magnetic film, used to fill gaps in FX or speech tracks and so avoid 'drop-outs'.

CLAPPER-BOARD
A board with information about the title, slate number and take number, which is filmed for a few frames at the start of every take, for identification purposes. A hinged arm at the top or side is swung closed with a smart clap for synchronization of picture and sound, when shooting sync.

COLOUR PILOT
With b/w cutting copies from colour original stock, a few frames from each take can be printed in colour for the editor to assess colour quality. The more usual procedure, however, is to order 10 per cent colour rushes, when the lab will extract 10 or 40 feet from each roll of film to print in colour, as a guide to colour quality in each roll.

COMMAG
Combined action and magnetic sound print; i.e. a married print with magnetic sound.

COMOPT
Combined action and optical sound print; i.e. a married print with optical sound.

CUT
The director's command to actor(s) or subject(s) and the cameraman, to finish.

CUT
The direct transition from one shot to another.

CUTAWAY
A shot related to the main action, but not directly part of it, which the editor can use to condense time, by cutting away from the main action and returning to a later stage of that action; or to cover faulty continuity, to conceal a missing shot or to use as a 'reaction shot' showing the reaction of a protagonist in the film, for example. On most kinds of film the cameraman will shoot a selection of cutaways, even if they are not specifically scripted.

CUTTING COPY
The print of the film upon which all the editing work is performed. It is usually taken from the rushes.

CUTTING POINT
The exact frame in the action where, in the editor's judgment, the cut to the subsequent shot, or from the preceding one, would be most effectively made.

DISSOLVE
See Mix.

DOLLY
A mobile support for the camera; usually a kind of three- or four-wheeled trolley; and often running on tracks.

DOLLY-SHOT
A shot taken with the camera moving on a dolly; more usually called a *tracking shot*.

DROP-OUT
A short period of complete silence on the sound-track caused by the omission of sound on all tracks; the absence of the slight background noise inherent in the recording process is immediately apparent. Such spaces are normally avoided by the use of 'fill' – see BUZZ.

DUBBING
Usually used to denote the mixing of sound-tracks to the mixed magnetic master, but is also used more loosely in connection with various kinds of sound transfer – e.g. dubbing on to magnetic stripe.

EDITING MACHINE
A machine that will run the picture and at least one separate sound-track together, at projection speed, and allow the editor to stop, re-run, reverse run, etc., and also gives easy access to the film to allow cutting.

EXCITER LAMP
The lamp on the projector that provides the beam of light which falls on the photo-electric cell in the optical sound-reading system.

EYELINE
The term, used in a number of closely connected connotations, which refers to the positioning of the camera during shooting so that when the resulting takes are projected, the illusion of spatial relationship of the objects or persons in the film corresponds to that at the actual scene of shooting.

FADE-IN
Where the picture gradually appears from a black screen until it is at full brightness. Usually denotes the start of a sequence.

FADE-OUT
The reverse of FADE-IN: the picture disappears to black. Usually the end of a sequence.

FOCUS-PULLING
The changing of focus during a take; either to keep the main subject in focus where it would otherwise not be so, or else to bring one object into focus where it had previously been out of focus (or vice versa) as a deliberate visual effect.

FORCING
The exposing of film at higher than its nominal speed-rating, and the extending of the development to compensate for this.

FRAME
The individual photographic image recorded on the film. There are twenty-four to each second of film running time at standard sound speed.

FREEZE-FRAME
An optical printer effect whereby at a chosen point in the action, the same frame is printed many times. This has the effect of stopping all movement, and producing a still photographic image. It is frequently used at the end of a film.

GEL
Abbreviation for 'gelatine filter', usually referring to large filters fitted over windows, for example, to adapt the colour temperature of daylight for mixed-lighting colour filming.

GEM MARKER
Strictly a trade-name, but widely used to refer to spirit markers which are much used for writing on film leaders, cans, etc.

GRADING
The assessment of the negative/master at the labs in order to programme the printer for the production of a consistent and high-quality print.

HIGH-KEY LIGHTING
Lighting of a scene so that all areas are brightly illuminated, and the brightness ratio is low.

JUMP-CUT
Any cut that jars badly on the screen; usually occurs when two succeeding images are similar enough for the dissimilarity to become jarring. A typical example is where the camera has stopped filming for a very short time and recommenced with the same lens; a few objects or people may have moved in relation to the identical background, and a direct jump from one position to another on the screen will occur. Jump-cuts can also be used positively, as a special effect.

LACING PATH
The path followed by the film through the camera or projector.

LATITUDE (of exposure)
The range of error of exposure within which it is still possible to produce acceptable prints from a given filmstock.

LEADER
Blank film, either clear or coated white or black (other colours are sometimes found) used for protecting the ends of rolls of film, or for spacing in sound or picture film rolls.

LEADERS
Specially marked lengths of film giving certain information and timing marks attached to the head and tail of rolls of film and projection prints. Usually coded by 'Academy' or SMPTE standards.

LOW-KEY LIGHTING
Lighting of a scene so that there are predominant areas of darkness contrasted with areas of highlight, with a high brightness ratio.

MAGNETIC STRIPE
An area of ferrous oxide recording medium coated down the non-sprocket side of a print which accepts the recording of the sound-track.

MARRIED PRINT
A finished print of a film which has the sound – either magnetic or optical – combined on to the same piece of film as the picture.

MATTE
A mask which prevents light reaching certain areas of the frame.

MATTE-BOX
Usually in the form of bellows in front of the camera lens, it accepts mattes and filters, holding them in front of the lens; it also acts as a lens-hood in many cameras.

MIX or DISSOLVE
Where one scene gradually changes to another on the screen. It is in fact the exact superimposition of a fade-in and a fade-out.

OPTICAL

A special effect made with the use of an optical printer, including wipes, freeze frames, reverse-runs, etc. Fades and dissolves are also usually referred to as opticals, although with modern printers and A & B roll assembly, they can be produced without recourse to the optical printer, and are sometimes not considered as true opticals.

OPTICAL MASTER/NEGATIVE

The photographic representation of the mixed magnetic master sound-track, as prepared in suitable form for printing on the final print of the film to produce an optical married print.

ORIGINAL

A term often used to denote the camera master film – the raw film stock that originally passed through the camera during the shooting of the film.

PAN

Abbreviation for 'panchromatic' – filmstock sensitive to light of all colours, as opposed to 'blue-sensitive'; sometimes used for making b/w prints from colour negative.

PAN

Abbreviation for 'panorama' – horizontal rotation of the camera round its vertical axis.

PERMAFILM

Protective treatment for film prints (trade-name).

PLAYOFF

Sound reproduction facility – e.g. disk playoff, tape-loop playoff, etc.

POLA-SCREEN

Polarizing filter, which cuts glare and reflection by the polarization of light rays – cf. 'Polaroid' sunglasses.

POLECAT

A support for lampheads: fits between ceiling and floor, and held firm by internal spring pressure.

PULSE-SYNC

System of retaining synchronization between picture and sound by recording a reference pulse from the camera on to the sound recording tape while shooting.

RELEASE PRINT

The final print of the film; the one that gets shown to the film's intended audience. With many films there may be only one print anyway, but on large print orders, final corrections to grading will have been sorted out in the ANSWER PRINT(S).

REVERSAL

A camera filmstock which, when processed in the correct way, produces a positive image.

'ROCK AND ROLL' or 'ROLL-BACK'

Describes sound-mixing facilities where all tracks can be run back in synchronization, allowing re-mixing (after a mistake or unsatisfactory balance, for example) to be undertaken sectionally. With older equipment it is necessary to return to the beginning of the rolls, re-establish sync, and re-mix the entire roll.

ROSTRUM

A camera mount that holds a camera (usually a special 'Rostrum camera') in a fixed relation to artwork on a level plane, and allows movement of both camera and the artwork. The rostrum is used chiefly for animation and titling work.

RUSHES

The initial quickly produced and usually ungraded print supplied by the labs when first developing the negative. The rushes normally become the cutting copy, or work-print.

SEPMAG

Separate magnetic sound-track, on 16 mm magnetic film.

SHOWPRINT

See Release print.

SHUSH

See Buzz.

SLATE

A shot of the film – a term used for identification purposes. Each shot will have a slate number and a take number. The slate number refers to the shot in the film, the take number refers to the number of the attempt to film it. Thus, slate 83, take 4 indicates that the shot in question is the fourth attempt to film shot number 83. The slate numbering may be either in script order, or shooting order.

SLATE

The clapper board.

SLATE (verb)

To mark the shot by exposing a few frames of film to the correctly marked slate.

SNOOT

A truncated cone-shaped attachment for photographic lamps; it produces a small round pool of illumination.

SPACING

Blank film used to fill out sound-tracks where magnetic film is not used.

SPACING, BLACK

Photographically opaque black film which is used chiefly to fill in alternate shot-lengths in A & B roll master assembly.

SPEED RATING

The index of the sensitivity of the filmstock's emulsion to light, usually reckoned on ASA or DIN scales. The higher the number, the 'faster' the film – i.e. the less light required to achieve a good exposure.

SPLICE

The join in the film. Splices are made either with transparent adhesive tape (especially in editing), or with cement (on master material or showprints).

STOP-PULLING

Altering the aperture of the lens during a take, usually to compensate for variations in illumination of the scene, especially during camera movements.

STRETCH PRINTING
An optical printer process where every alternate frame is printed twice. The chief application of this technique is in preparing film shot at 16 f.p.s. for projection at sound speed without speeding up the apparent motion of the content.

STRIKE FRAME
The frame of the picture film where the arm of the clapper-board first makes contact with the body of the slate; on the sound film, the frame which contains the first sound of the resulting noise. The sound and picture strike frames are lined up for synchronization of action and sound.

SUN-GUN
A small, portable photographic lamp of high efficiency and low weight. Can be operated either from mains or battery.

TAKE
See Slate.

TILT
The vertical equivalent of the PAN: a movement of the camera about its horizontal axis. The term 'pan' is often used to cover a tilt.

TRACK
The rails laid down to guide a dolly smoothly along the required path. Hence *tracking shot, track in, track out*. The abbreviated form *track* is often used to stand for *tracking shot*.

TRACK
Sound-track. Hence *music-track, sync-track, FX-track*, etc.

TRACK-LAYING
The compilation of the sound-tracks, normally on separate 16 mm mag. film.

TURN OVER
The director's command to commence running of the camera and/or the sound recorder.

UPRATING
See Forcing.

VOICEOVER
A non-sync voice on the sound-track which might be supposed to be coming from one of the protagonists of the film; more loosely, any substantial section of spoken sound-track other than a formal commentary.

WHITE-OUT
The fading of the image to a white screen: a fade-out to white.

WILD SOUND
Sound shot non-synchronously.

WIPE
An optical printer effect where the incoming shot replaces the outgoing shot on the screen without any mixing or superimposition. The wipe can be produced in many styles – either with straight edges moving in any direction across the screen, or with the new picture appearing from the centre, or the edges of the screen.

WORKPRINT
Cutting copy.

WOW
Distortion of sound in recording process, caused by uneven speed in the transport system of the recording or playback machinery. The effect is of inconsistency of pitch, and is especially noticeable with music.

Further reading

American Cinematographer Manual.

American Cinematographer 16/35 Cameraman Handbook.

ANDERSON, L.: Making a Film. London, 1952.

BADDELEY, W.H.: Technique of Documentary Film Production. New York and London, 1963.

BRANSTON, B.: A Film Maker's Guide to Planning, Directing and Shooting Films for Pleasure and Profit. New York, 1968.

BRUNEL, A.: Filmcraft. London, 1933.

BURDER, J.: The Technique of Editing 16 mm. Films. London and New York, 1968.

CAMPBELL, R.: Photographic Theory for the Motion Picture Cameraman. London, 1971.

CAMPBELL, R.: Practical Motion Picture Photography. Cranbury, N.J., and London, 1971.

DABORN, J.: Cine Titling. Hemel Hempstead, Herts, 1960.

FERGUSON, R.: How to Make Movies: a practical guide to group film making. New York, 1969.

Filmatic Data Sheets (latest techniques in processing). Filmatic Laboratories Ltd, Lonsdale Road, London, W11.

FISHER, J.D. (ed.): The Craft of Film. London, 1970.

GIBSON, B.: Exposing Cine Film. Hemel Hempstead, Herts, 1960.

GROVES, P.D.: Film in Higher Education and Research. Elmsford, N.Y., and Oxford, 1966.

HAPPÉ, L.B.: Basic Motion Picture Technology. London, 1971.

LEVITAN, E.L.: An Alphabetical Guide to Motion Picture, Television and Videotape Production. New York, 1970.

LOWNDES, D.: Film Making in Schools. London, 1968; New York, 1969.

MANVELL, R., and J. HUNTLEY: The Technique of Film Music. London and New York, 1957.

MARNER, T.StJ.: Directing Motion Pictures. Cranbury, N.J., and London, 1972.

NISBETT, A.: The Technique of the Sound Studio. London, 1969; New York, 1970.

PINCUS, E.: Guide to Film Making. New York, 1969.

REISZ, K., and G. MILLAR: The Technique of Film Editing. New York, 1967; London, 1968.

REYNERTSON, A.J.: The Work of the Film Director. New York, 1970.

RILLA, W.: A-Z of Movie Making. New York, 1970.

ROSENTHAL, A.: The New Documentary in Action. Berkeley, Calif., 1971.

SMALLMAN, K.: Creative Film-making. New York, 1969.

SOUTO, H.M.R.: The Technique of the Motion Picture Camera. New York, 1967.

SPOTTISWOODE, R.: Film and its Techniques. London, 1968; Berkeley, Calif., 1951.

SPOTTISWOODE, R. (ed.): Focal Encyclopaedia of Film and Television Techniques. New York, 1969.

SURGENOR, A.J.: Bolex H16-H8 Guide. London and New York, 1967.

WALTER, E.: The Technique of the Film Cutting Room. New York, 1969.

WHEELER, L.J.: Principles of Cinematography. London, 1969.

(NB: New editions of these works are often available; dates given are those of the latest editions at the time of going to press.)

JOURNALS

American Cinematographer, monthly.
ASC Agency Inc., 1782 North Grange Drive, Hollywood, California 90028.

Audio Visual, monthly.
Current Affairs Ltd, PO Box 109, Croydon CR9 1QH.

British Journal of Photography, weekly.
Henry Greenwood & Co. Ltd, 24 Wellington Street, London WC2E 7DG.

British Kinematography, Sound and Television, monthly.
BKST Society, 110–112 Victoria House, Vernon Place, London WC1.

Film Making, monthly.
Fraser Pearce Ltd, Wessex House, 26 Station Road, Cambridge CB1 2LB.

Movie Maker, monthly.
Model and Allied Publication Ltd, Station Road, King's Langley, Herts.

SMPTE Journal, monthly.
Society of Motion Picture and Television Engineers, 9E. 41st St., New York, N.Y. 10017.

Index